GOLF

HOW TO PLAY EACH SHOT BY THE PROFESSIONALS

•DENIS MACHENAUD•

Grange BOOKS

LE GOLF – UNE PASSION
© Edition de la Martiniere, Paris, France

English-language edition
© 1996 Transedition Ltd, Oxford, England

Photographic credits: Dye Designs,
Denis Machenaud, X
Illustrations: Thierry Mysius

This edition published in the UK in 1996 by
Grange Books PLC,
an imprint of Grange Books PLC,
The Grange, Grange Yard,
London SE1 3AG

Printed in 1996 in China

ISBN 1 85627 873 5 – Golf

CONTENTS

PREFACE

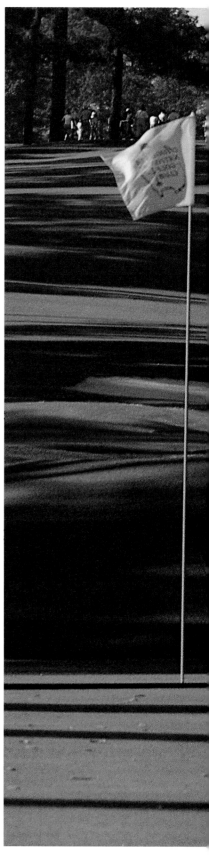

Golf: How to Play Each Shot By The Professionals is a work on technique. Essential, uncomplicated technique, that is. One might ask what could possibly be added to what has already been propounded, with such skill, by the great Ben Hogan in 1957, when he wrote his masterpiece *The Fundamentals of Golf*. Surely, everything had been said, and it could have been left at that? But if the theory has hardly changed, methods of teaching certainly have. Today the beginner learns, club in hand, far more quickly than he or she would have done thirty years ago. This is because a player is now taught to understand the basic principles of the golf swing, rather than learning through trial and error.

A theoretical example is not sufficient to give real understanding. The pupil must develop a mental image. It is often said that "Words vanish into thin air," while in contrast, visualizing what has to be done becomes imprinted on the brain and remains. What modern teaching has achieved is to guide the learner through a more personalized, and therefore more appropriate method. There is no single method of teaching golf, but several. This fact is both reassuring and worrying at the same time!

Golfers frequently declare that they are confused as to which advice they should follow and are nervous because, "the simple act of changing my teacher throws into question a golf swing that I've spent months, even years, working on." If there is often an element of exaggeration among those who are having difficulty in making progress, there is still enormous frustration at what seems to be an impossible subject. More than in other sports, it appears, golfers suffer from "good days" and "bad days." When things are going well, golf can seem the simplest of games. But when a single grain of sand puts a spanner in the works – and this happens several times on each course – confidence vanishes, and it's as if you've never picked up a club in your life. This can happen just as easily after ten years of practice as after the first lesson. How does one explain the fact that even the greatest exponents of the game are capable of compiling scores in the 80s? Especially considering all the vast technical know-how they have?

However you play the game, feel is the one essential in the game of golf. Nothing disappears more quickly than the glorious, fleeting feeling of hitting a good shot. Added to this, the perfectly struck shot is hard to explain, while there are generally a hundred reasons for a bad shot.

In attempting to commit the basics of the swing to memory, it is important not only to be absolutely clear about the "fundamentals," but also to put all the unstintingly given advice into practice. One of the great "swing gurus" currently in vogue is Florida-based David Leadbetter. He believes that practice routines, or "drills," are necessary in order to perfect a swing. They enable players to work on particular aspects of their game and, importantly, create feel by virtue of their repetition.

During the ten years that I have worshiped at the altar of the little white ball, I have come across very few works – if any – which bring together in one volume all the multitudinous practice exercises and the myriad advice aimed at simplifying the learning process. Long practice sessions can be discouraging. On the other hand, if one regards practice as fun, everything becomes much easier. The accomplished player with a scratch handicap, every bit as much as the beginner or average player can benefit greatly from these "300 tips for making progress." What is wonderful about golf is that anyone can play it. Somewhere in the world there exists a championship for blind golfers, and another for people with one arm. Everyone can make progress. A serious golfer will not ask "How?" but "How many?" In other words, it's the end result which matters. Ultimately the means count for little. Learning to swing a club with your feet strapped together and a belt around your arms, or to practice putting blindfolded may sound purely anecdotal. I can assure you that they are not, as I've been there! Look at the champions with near-infallible technique. They too believe in all kinds of little "tricks of the trade" which help them achieve a steady, balanced swing. It would be silly not to try out a few of them, wouldn't it?

DENIS MACHENAUD

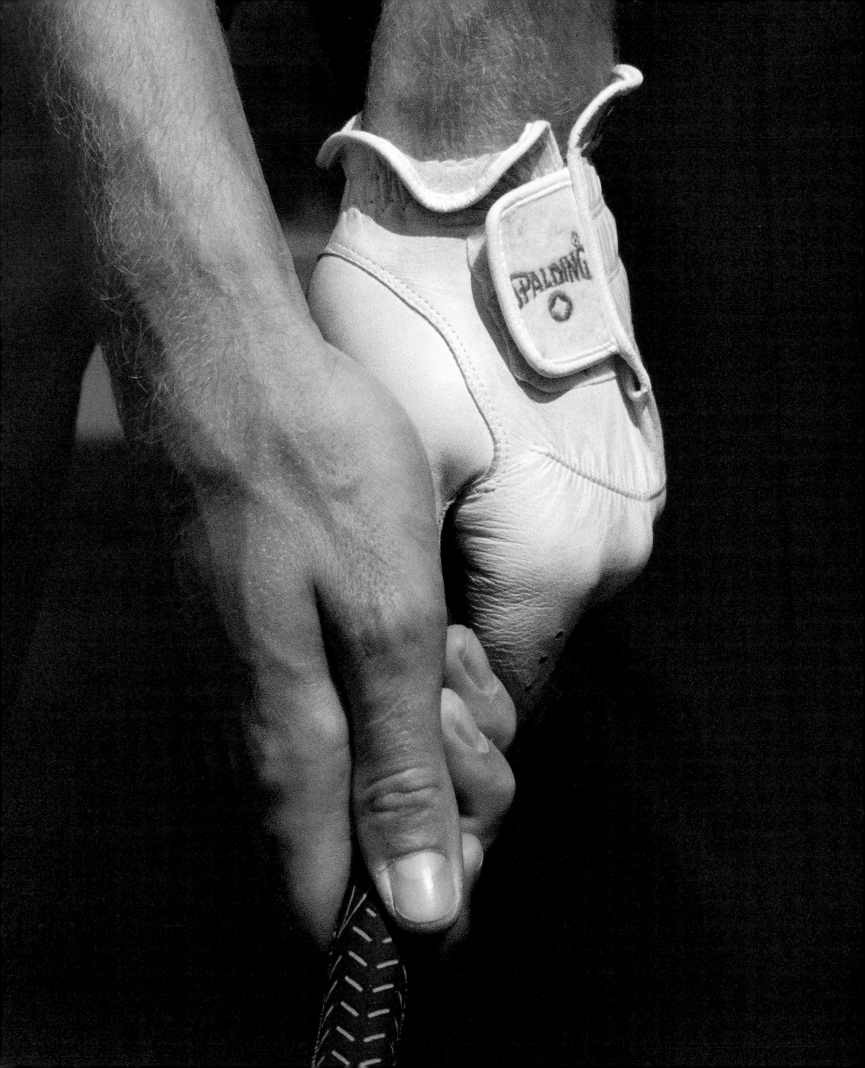

THE GRIP

The history of the grip is lost in the mists of time. To research it, one would need to trace the very beginnings of golf itself, and journey to an age when the first golfers took hold of a golf club and attempted to hit a crude version of the golf ball we know today. The main development in the grip has been related partly to changing fashions, as advocated by certain champions, and also to the evolution of golfing equipment in general.

Just for a moment, imagine that you have a hickory-shafted club in your hands, i.e. a wooden shaft, and you are ready to hit a ball, which is made of gutta-percha. Difficult! Yet our predecessors had to cope with this situation. It wasn't so much the wooden shaft which caused problems, but rather the texture of the ball. To take the impact of hitting a gutta-percha ball, the grip needed to be much more firm than the kind we encourage today. As for the method of holding the shaft, the most natural way was in the palm of the hands, with both thumbs round the shaft as opposed to only on top. This kind of "baseball grip," which went perfectly with the swing of the time, called the "St. Andrew's swing," involved significant rotation of the body, lots of sway, strong leg action and plenty of wrist movement at impact. Like today, there were already variations on this grip. Some people held the club predominantly in the palm of the left hand and used only the fingers of the right hand. Others

THERE IS NO SINGLE
CORRECT GRIP, BUT
SEVERAL.
TRY OUT THE VARIOUS
ALTERNATIVES AND
TAKE YOUR TIME. THE
GRIP IS A VERY
PERSONAL THING.

held the shaft with the right hand, either exaggeratedly underneath or on top. In short, confusion reigned, which led inevitably to the arrival of two new methods, known as the "interlocking grip" and the "overlapping grip."

Around the turn of the century, three golfers dominated the game: – Harry Vardon, J.H. Taylor and James Braid – or the "Great Triumvirate" as they were called. Between 1894 and 1914, they won 21 British Opens between them. All three used the new modern grip, characterized by the thumb position lying more on the shaft, plus a more obvious hold with the fingers. This grip, initially named the "overlapping grip," came to be known as the "Vardon grip."

In 1898, an American from Cleveland, Cobrun Haskell, invented the rubber ball, which differed from the existing ball in its greater shock resistance. Its effect was to revolutionize the grip. The hold on the shaft became lighter and nearly all golfers adopted the overlapping grip as well as the very upright swing used by Harry Vardon. Only a few players dissented, the most famous of these being Gene Sarazen who preferred the interlocking grip, which he used to win seven major championships in the 1920s and 1930s. Today, the overlapping grip is the most common.

The *overlapping grip* is characterized by the position of the little finger of the right hand, which is placed above the index finger and middle finger of the left hand on the shaft. Naturally, the right hand is below the left hand on the shaft.

The *interlocking grip* has the most famous adherent in Jack Nicklaus. The variation in relation to the overlapping grip lies in the position of the little finger on the right hand, which in this case fits in between the index and middle fingers of the left hand.

Finally, the *two-handed grip*, also called the baseball grip, allows the possibility of all ten fingers resting on the shaft, but care must be taken not to create a gap between the two hands. This grip often produces a longer drive but less compactness than the first two.

How do you hold the club?

Why do most golfers wear a glove when playing, and why are these gloves so prone to wear and tear? Undoubtedly it is because the pressure exerted by the left hand on the club is very significant; indeed, so significant that many

THE GRIP

CHECK YOUR GRIP BEFORE YOU START TO PLAY.
MANY AMATEURS FAIL TO PAY DUE ATTENTION TO IT.

HOLD THE CLUB TIGHTLY

If you have a light grip, just consider how you shake hands with a friend. Lay the sole of the club flat on the ground, perpendicular to the line of flight, and hold the end of the shaft with your right hand.

Imagine that you are shaking hands with someone, then lower your arm and left hand together to pick up the shaft, taking care to lay the thumb on the top part of the shaft. Once the left hand is in position, the right hand will follow easily.

GRIPPING A PIECE OF WOOD

A good way of getting a feel for the correct grip is to use a square piece of wood. Place the left thumb on the right side of the wood and the right thumb on the left corner. The V formed by the thumbs and index fingers should point towards the right shoulder.

USE TOOTHPASTE INSTEAD OF A CLUB ▶

In order to suggest how much pressure should be exerted on the club shaft by the hands, the image of a bird held in the hand often comes to mind. It was the legendary Sam Snead who first described a light grip by using such a comparison.

Another good analogy is with a tube of toothpaste: if you press too hard, you risk squeezing out too much of the toothpaste. Your hands, forearms and top of the body should be completely relaxed.

players are obliged to change their glove frequently when holes appear in the same place, i.e. in the lower part of the palm. These players tend to be over-enthusiastic beginners who exert excessive pressure on the club, which unfortunately only leads to bad results.

The grip is the poor relation of the golf swing and wrongly so. Like a car whose gearbox and transmission system are not checked, the hands are the only link with the club, and they channel the energy from the arms and body. If the grip is correct, there is a good chance that the swing will at least work, even if it is far from perfect. If the grip is wrong, considerable compensation is needed to enable the ball to be hit correctly.

Many amateur players, however, attach little importance to the grip, and rarely consider it as the source of their problems. Perhaps the grip is not as "interesting" as the swing itself but it needs just as much attention.

The definition of the word "grip" can be summed up as, "the position of the hands on the shaft of the club." Two things enable the quality of a shot to be judged: power and direction. These are determined by the position of the hands on the shaft. The power, due mainly to the body action, is transmitted to the club via the hands. The

LEFT HAND

To achieve the correct grip, ask yourself whether your left hand, like the clubface, is perpendicular to the target. In other words, the back of the left hand should be parallel with the target.

GRIP THE CLUB ON THE GROUND

When you check your grip, it is better if the club is resting on the ground. In this way, it is also easier to align the hands in relation to the clubface and the club in relation to the target.

trajectory of the ball is essentially determined by the angle at which the clubface hits the ball.

To take up your grip, you should place the club blade square to the ground, i.e. perpendicular in relation to the target. First, place the left hand at the top of the shaft. The club is lying diagonally on the palm. The first three fingers hold the shaft firmly. The thumb lies on the top. If the fingers were around the shaft instead of being diagonal, the left thumb would tend to be too far back, which may lead to lack of control in the swing.

The right hand partially covers the left hand. The palm is placed on the shaft at the height of the left thumb. The middle and ring fingers hold the shaft firmly. The little finger fits between the index and middle fingers of the left hand. The thumb is on the shaft. The index finger is under the shaft.

The next part is very important: the thumb and index finger of the left hand should form a V, the point of which should lie between the chin and the right shoulder. To ascertain whether the left hand grip is correct, only the first two knuckle joints and part of the third should be visible. When the left hand is in the correct position, there is a 90 percent chance of the right hand being correct too. To insure that your grip is

sound, it is best not to have the club resting on the ground.

Forming a grip requires a sequence of movements, just like the golf swing. First the left hand, then the right. But why place the left hand on the club first? Simply because the left arm leads the swing, or the left arm and hand to be more precise. Experts will tell you that the swing is a pendulum movement, whose base point is the shoulders. In spite of this somewhat disconcerting logic, it should be said that the majority of beginners hold the club with their right hand if they are right-handed. They think that they will hit the ball better in this way. But the golf swing is essentially a throwing action, and this is very important. If you do not grasp this, the golf swing is impossible to understand.

When children start to play they tend immediately to adopt a very "strong" grip, i.e. with the left hand turned towards the right of the shaft. This is understandable – their hands are not strong enough to grip the club squarely. They hold the club better in this way. It is not advisable, however, and should be quickly discouraged before it becomes a bad habit. This remark is valid for all golfers. Even if you have to suffer at the start, it will be worth it. The grip is

WHERE GOOD LUCK STARTS

If you find that you are regularly hitting a slice, ask yourself whether an incorrect grip is the reason. It often happens that the grip with the right hand is too loose, making you grip the club tighter in the downswing, forcing you to swing at the ball with an outside-to-inside trajectory. To put this right, put a coin between the base of the right and left thumbs. If it falls to the ground, you haven't maintained constant pressure during the swing. You know what you have to do.

THE TOWEL SHOT ▶

If you are told, or if you feel that your grip is too tight, so increasing the risk of over-emphasizing the hands, take a towel and wrap it around the club grip. Now try to play like this, forgetting about the towel. Your grip will become less tight.

THE RARE PLEASURE OF
FINDING ONESELF ALONE
ON A LINKS COURSE WITH
ONLY THE NEARBY
OCEAN FOR A
COMPANION. THIS
PHOTOGRAPH SHOWS
THE LINKS COURSE AT
ROYAL ABERDEEN IN THE
NORTH EAST OF
SCOTLAND.

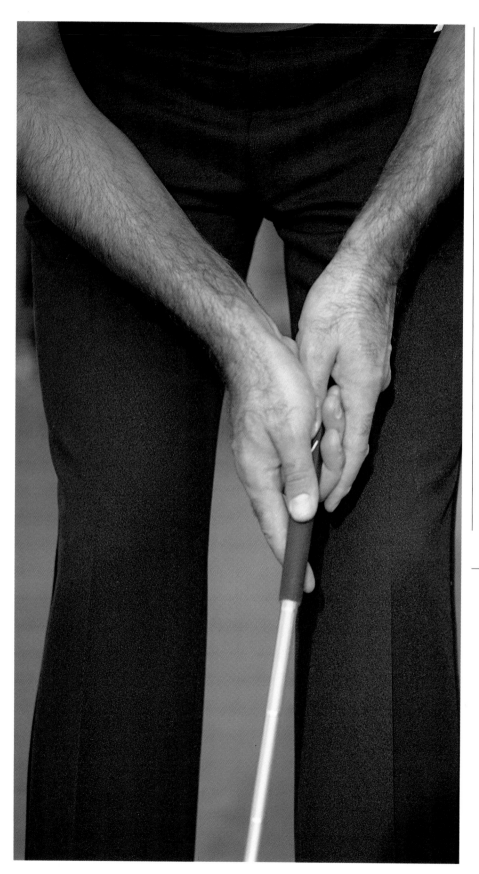

not a problem which is specific to beginners. Even the finest players experience occasional difficulties with their grip. The first lessons are decisive, as it becomes very hard to change later. It is exactly the same with learning to play the piano. The way the fingers are first laid on the piano keys greatly influences the pianist's future career.

What about the pressure of the hands on the shaft?

The left hand directs the movement and orientates the club face in relation to the flag, and the right hand controls the weight of the club. Each has its role to play, even if they are condemned to work together! The left hand takes approximately 80 percent of the pressure. This is to be expected, as it brings the club downward, while the right hand is more in tow, and takes the remaining 20 percent. To get a good feel for the hand action, try swinging without a club. This will make you more aware of your hands and of their speed at impact.

One way to achieve a good grip is to develop the muscles in your fingers by suitable, simple

THIS IS THE GRIP USED
BY EUROPE'S MOST
FAMOUS GOLFER,
SEVERIANO
BALLESTEROS. HE GRIPS
THE CLUB LESS FIRMLY
WHEN PUTTING, AS IF HE
WERE HOLDING A BIRD
IN HIS HAND.

exercises such as squeezing a rubber ball as many times as possible. Check your grip regularly. You will need patience and perseverance.

What you mustn't do: move the left thumb to the right or left sides of the shaft; or have your right hand "open" on the right side of the shaft; or hold the shaft in the fingers of the left hand and not sufficiently in the palms; or lack firmness in the pressure of the three fingers of the left hand: middle, ring and little fingers, and the two fingers on the right hand: middle and ring fingers.

In addition to the basic methods of grip dealt with above, there are three different ways of placing your hands on the club, and it depends on what you are trying to do.

The Strong Grip

If you want more distance, even to the detriment of some accuracy, or if you want to draw the ball (from right to left), try this grip. Place your left hand nearer the top of the shaft, with the right hand beneath. The V formed by the thumbs and the index finger should point toward the right shoulder. It should then be possible to see three knuckle joints on the left hand when addressing the ball. The trajectory of the movement should be more inside-to-outside, with the ball flying lower, from right to left, with more wrist action and more distance.

If the ball is positioned below the level of your feet, the tendency will be to slice it (left-right effect). If you change your grip, you should be able to play the ball to the right. Squeeze the shaft more tightly with both hands, particularly the left one. You will use your wrists more. The grip should be stronger with the left hand turned slightly to the right. To keep your balance, put more weight on your heels.

The Neutral Grip

In eliminating wrist action, you risk losing a little length in favor of more accuracy. So the hands should be placed squarely on the club, so that the V points toward the chin and right eye. You should be able to see two knuckle joints on the left hand.

The Weak Grip

This is the grip to use for greater accuracy. Turn your left hand to the left under the shaft, with the right hand above it. The V should point at the chin, and you will not be able to see the two joints

CHECK YOUR GRIP

A good way of checking if you have the correct grip is to hold the club normally without any particular pressure, then raise it to shoulder height. Now squeeze your grip tightly – if the club-face moves and turns, you can be sure that the same thing will happen on impact. You will not reduce the pressure operating on the club during the swing, but what you must avoid is movement of the clubface. You need to adapt your grip if this happens.

A TEE IN THE RIGHT HAND

It is generally the right hand which is incorrectly positioned on the club when addressing the ball. You can check it by putting a tee in the hollow of the hand between the thumb and index finger. If you have the correct grip, the tee will face the right shoulder. If your grip is too strong, the tee will point to the right and if it is too weak, it will point toward you.

THE CHAIR TEST

Players often close the clubface during the backswing, open it upon impact and generally fail to use their hands and forearms correctly due to the wrong grip. Likely results: a lofted slice with a wood; a thinned approach shot with a short iron; and reduced clubhead speed. This is because the club is held too much in the palm of the hand. Solution: adopt another more natural grip, using the fingers more.

To get the actual feel of the hands and forearm action, take a chair (out onto the golf course if possible!) and sit down. Now set up a ball and hit it. By practicing this, the club will travel better than before, moving clockwise in the backswing and anticlockwise during the downswing. You will then follow-through from the inside. Ideally the shoulders and torso should be locked.

on the left hand so easily. The trajectory of the ball will be a left-to-right fade, and higher, as the ball is being hit at a more vertical angle.

If the ball is positioned above the level of your feet, you will tend to hook it. To avoid this, modify your grip. Grip more strongly with the left hand to keep the club face square upon impact. Use a "weak" grip, turning your hands slightly to the left. To maintain balance, put more weight on your toes.

The Light Grip

If you need to hit a ball up over a tree, or in the direction of a raised green, for example, the best way to achieve this is to use a light, flexible grip. This technique allows maximum wrist action and gives the ball a lot of spin. The club is essentially maneuvred by the hands and arms. Your stance should be as narrow as possible.

The Firm Grip

If your ball is buried in thick rough, use a firm grip with little or no wrist action. Apply pressure with both hands firmly on the club, generate slower club speed but stronger body action. The stance is wider with a little more weight on the left side.

Grip errors

There are various grip errors, varying with the level of the player.

The strong grip: when your hands are too far to the right, with four knuckles visible, there is often a lack of power, with the forearms turning to the left on the downswing in a more neutral position, causing the clubface to be closed.

The weak grip: this often gives rise to a slice. On the downswing, the forearms turn to the right and open up the clubface.

The hands act separately: for example, it sometimes happens that in spite of, or because of, the right hand being placed under the club in a "strong" position, shots go low and to the right. Generally speaking, a grip with the right hand turned to the right causes a hook. But often the result is the opposite, as when the wrists lock on impact. The tee test described in this chapter should enable you to position the right hand better when addressing the ball and to allow it to operate normally during the swing.

Sometimes the right hand is turned too far to the left, with the palm facing the ground. This position is too weak and prevents squareness upon impact. The action of the top half of the

MISTY, EARLY MORNING
GOLF AT VALESCURE IN
THE SOUTH OF FRANCE.

body is too strong on the downswing, the hands are not strong enough and the clubface remains open. Result: a slice. Remedy: turn your right hand more to the left of the shaft so that the palm is aimed toward the target and not toward the ground.

When to change your grip?

There are many ways to correct a poor grip, but the first stage is to be able to identify a grip error and realize that it may be the reason for a bad shot.

If the ball has excessive spin, (of whatever nature) there may be:
– lack of power and bad follow-through upon impact;
– excessive tension in the arms and top half of the body when addressing the ball and during the swing;
– a shortened backswing due to a lack of suppleness and wrist action;
– shanking;
– pronounced overswing.

All these factors can be explained by an incorrect grip.

SEVERIANO BALLESTEROS AGAIN: NOTE THE IMPECCABLE STANCE WHEN ADDRESSING THE BALL, WITH HIS EYE ON THE TARGET; ALSO THE PERFECT GRIP, WITH THE LEFT HAND CORRECTLY PLACED ON THE SHAFT AND THE RIGHT HAND BELOW IT.

Various studies have been carried out, advising the use of different grips according to your build, suppleness, age, etc. *Here are some conclusions:*
– the neutral grip: recommended for good players (handicap of less than 15) and also for powerful players;
– three or four knuckles visible on the left hand: recommended for players with a high handicap, for those with limited strength, juniors and women of a good standard;
– a light grip using the fingers more: recommended for slicers, seniors, tense players or those lacking power;
– the interlocking grip: for players with small hands, juniors and women;
– the two-handed grip: for players lacking power, seniors and beginner juniors.

The best advice of all, though, is to search until you find a grip which suits you. The aim is to find a grip which is beneficial to you, enabling the clubface to strike the ball squarely upon impact.

The two-handed grip

This grip is not often used, but it has some good points, and will appeal to a lot of golfers. It used to be called the "St. Andrew's grip" but now, for obvious reasons, it is known as the "baseball grip."

It is recommended for golfers who lack power, for juniors and for many women players.

It is characterized by greater control of the club, with eight fingers placed directly on the shaft, as against seven in the overlapping grip and six in the interlocking grip. When people pick up a club for the first time, they pick it up in this way.

Advantages: greater maneuverability of the club; more "feel" because the fingers of the right hand are in full contact with the club, which is very important in the short game; easier wrist action and therefore greater clubhead speed; better follow-through with good hand movement.

How to hold the club: it is different from the two other main grips, the overlapping and interlocking grips, as it is not the palm of the right hand but the fingers which lie on the shaft. It is easier to get the right hand square and less underneath the shaft.

Disadvantages: it is said that the two-handed grip does not allow the compactness of the traditional grip; the hands are less closely linked. Significantly, although widely in use at the turn of the century, no great player uses this method today.

THE "CATHEDRAL IN THE PINES": AUGUSTA NATIONAL, WHERE THE MASTERS TOURNAMENT IS HELD EACH SPRING.

SET UP, ALIGNMENT, STANCE

Golfers often say that it is possible to predict the outcome of a golf shot even before it has been executed. This is due to the fact that because the golf swing is very much a sequence, the end result can be deduced from the set up. Like the grip, certain fundamental principles apply to setting up which cannot be ignored without bringing serious disappointment. It is certainly extremely difficult to automate. We don't wake up every day in the same physical shape, and our feelings are equally divergent. Although this in itself shouldn't stop us from having the same discipline before making every swing!

"Setting up" comprises both aspects of the address, i.e. posture and alignment. Broadly speaking, posture in golf relates to the position of the feet on the ground and to the general body position. The position of the feet, i.e. the "stance," is fundamental, since it conditions the general body position and therefore the future flight of the ball.

A BALL, A TEE AND A CLUB. WHAT COULD BE MORE SIMPLE TO MASTER? BUT APPEARANCES ARE DECEPTIVE. THIS PHOTO CAPTURES A CRUCIAL MOMENT, AS EVEN A SLIGHT VARIATION IN THE POSITION OF THE CLUB IN RELATION TO THE TARGET IS ENOUGH TO MAKE THE BALL DEVIATE BY SEVERAL YARDS.

SCOTLAND'S SAM TORRANCE, IN FULL CRY DURING THE BRITISH OPEN AT TURNBERRY. HIS POSITION AT IMPACT IS EXCELLENT – BUT THEN SO WAS HIS POSITION AT ADDRESS.

The ideal, or classic stance is square, with the two feet in a line parallel to the line of flight. If the left foot is slightly behind, an open stance is effected. This stance is especially relevant should you want to put spin on the ball, and also for short shots. Alternatively, if the right foot is a little behind the line, a closed stance is produced; this is rarely used, except in error or to facilitate spin.

The body position or "posture" should be as natural and comfortable as possible. It is important to align the feet, knees (lightly flexed), hips and shoulders accurately, and to lean the chest forwards slightly while keeping the back straight. The arms should fall naturally in front of the body. The head is kept still up to (and beyond) the moment of impact.

These are the principles. The reality is often different! There are at least FIVE common faults:
– weight too much on the heels. Back too stiff. Legs and knees too flexed. Result: the club rotates too quickly inside the line at the start of the backswing. The shoulders turn too "flat";
– too much weight on the toes. Back too bent. Legs too stiff. Result: the club rises outside the line and the shoulders turn too steeply;
– weight distribution too much to the left. Shoulders are open and pointing to the left.

Result: the club rises too much outside the line and too vertically, producing a pull, a slice and even fluffing;
– arms too stiff. Result: the top of the body is too taut, creating a poor pivot;
– stance too wide or too narrow. Result: poor rotation, poor weight transfer, loss of balance.

A correct address position is important in two ways:
– good posture gives the player enough space for his arms and club, and these can be moved without hindrance from the body;
– the correct position of the arms, feet and ball guarantees that the clubface will make contact with the ball just before the lowest point of the swing arc.

Generally, golfers tend not to stand straight enough when setting up. The mental image of the golfer in an armchair is often used to help visualize a good position, although this is often taken too literally, and the result is often the opposite of what is intended. A lot of people try to recreate a sitting position, with poor results. They are often too close to the ball and their movement is too cramped. The reason is simple: instead of bending the upper body from the top of the thighs, they lean forward from the stomach. It is

A SINGLE LINE

It is of the greatest importance to follow the same, and preferably the best setting up procedure every time. It's what the champions do. For this reason, you must follow certain essential principles: the alignment of the left hand with the shaft of the club – together they should form a single line – and the wrists should never be bent or in opposing directions. If the shaft of the club is inclined, the player's hands will tend to be behind the ball, causing him to lock his wrists from the start of the backswing.

THE TEE IN FRONT

The importance of playing from a tee should not be overlooked. It makes the stroke easier and longer, particularly when using a driver. With a wood, the strike is executed laterally and sometimes even at the beginning of the follow-through. As the driver is the least open club, it is vital to situate the tee well in front, at least at the height of the left heel. The driver will then hit the ball at the lowest point in its trajectory.

THE RIGHT ELBOW IN THE SET UP

The position of the right elbow has a considerable influence on the backswing arc. It should not touch the body, but should remain very close to it. It should be under the left elbow which is straight. The right elbow must be flexible and supple.

A STRAIGHT BACK ▶

To be sure of having a good address position, in terms of the back in particular, take a wedge and lay it on your back, with the clubhead pointing down in the right hand. Then bend your knees and lean forward from the waist, insuring that the grip of the club touches your head.

FOR A GOOD SHOULDER POSITION

When setting up, the left shoulder should always be higher than the right. To make sure, set up in stages: first, place the club behind the ball and hold the club with the left hand only; secondly, grip with the right hand. When you take the club with the right hand, the right shoulder should drop slightly. The left arm is straight, while the right is slightly bent and closer to the body.

AND THE HEAD?

Few golfers believe that they move their head during the swing. But an awful lot do. To find out if you do, ask a friend to put a club above your head. The slightest movement will be apparent. Obviously the club should remain on the head throughout the backswing.

LOOK IN THE MIRROR

Sometimes it is useful to look in to a mirror to examine whether your setting up position is correct. Mirrors are often used in practice sessions.

IF YOU STILL AREN'T SURE

There is another way to check whether or not your head moves during the swing. In the evening, as shadows begin to appear, lay a hat or cap in the place where the shadow of your head is formed. When you hit some shots, it should be easy to see if the shadow moves or not, and to work out the consequences.

HANDS AT THE TOP OF THE CLUB

For most golfers, the left hand should be about a hand's width from the body at address. With the driver, the little finger of the left hand should be about 8 inches (20 cm) from the body. This distance decreases accordingly if you use a shorter club. If you are not sure, a friend can check the distance for you.

THE LEFT HAND LEADS

The left hand controls and determines the position of the clubface. When adopting a stance, you should always try to align the left hand exactly, and to do so, your grip needs to be absolutely right. If this is not the case, the clubface will be wrongly aligned. As far as possible, keep control of the left hand throughout the swing.

important to maintain correct balance. Weight should be distributed evenly.

Ball position

Although we often complicate the procedure, the theory is easy to understand.

It is the left arm that leads the swing and determines the swing arc. The more the shot is to be made on the downswing, i.e. the shorter the club, the further the ball should be from the left foot in order to reach the midpoint of the stance. The ball should be struck just before the club reaches the lowest point of the swing.

The advantage of keeping the ball in practically the same position is that the swing does not need to be modified. It is, in fact, the stance which must change, not the position of the ball. For a short shot, the stance is narrower, and that's all there is to it. In any case, the margin for maneuvering the ball is reduced. Its position varies from being an extension of the left heel with a driver to being in the middle of the stance when playing a wedge. However, when spin is required i.e. when a shot is to be shaped, the ball must be positioned accordingly.

Alignment

There is nothing more frustrating than hitting a shot which falls 20 or 30 yards (20–30 m) short of the target. If the ball has been hit well, this can only be explained by bad alignment.

Alignment is therefore vitally important if you want to hit a good shot. It is important to follow the same routine before playing each shot. Watch the champions. It is interesting to see how each prepares in his or her own way, but always with the same principles in mind.

If you have ever fired a gun or a rifle at a range, then first you must have lined yourself up to hit the target. You aimed the gun at the target; and lined up the barrel accordingly. It's the same in golf. Too many golfers stand in front of the ball without thinking. There are three things which must be done. First, identify where the target is and align yourself properly. To do this, stand behind the ball and identify the line between it and the target, this will give you a reference point for the alignment of the clubface and body. Next you place the clubface at right angles to the target and then, and only then, assume your stance.

Apparently inexplicable errors occur simply because ball position and alignment are not

THE HIGH TEE ▶

When driving off, position the tee so that the top half of the ball is higher than the clubhead which at this moment (you are setting up) is on the ground. It is important to hit when the club begins to rise again. If the tee is too low, the club will "top" the ball and you will hook or slice. If the tee is too high, the ball will be hit underneath and you will sky it and it will go short.

TO ACQUIRE GOOD POSTURE

This is a good exercise to help you to set up correctly: stand with a club in your hand about 6 inches (15 cm) behind the ball and shadow your swing. Then, without stopping, go toward the ball and actually play it. You will quickly feel what the correct sensation is.

PLAYING IS WALKING

When we walk we take regular steps. So when you are setting up, think of the span of your step. Your stance should not be wider than the normal length of your step.

MAKE YOUR STANCE NARROWER

It is better to have a narrow stance than one which is too wide.

To find a good swing rhythm, balance your arms better and turn your shoulders better, and lastly, to control the ball better, make your stance narrower.

THE SHORT BUT TALENTED WELSH PLAYER, IAN WOOSNAM. HERE HE DEMONSTRATES A PERFECT POSITION AT THE TOP OF THE BACKSWING – THE RESULT OF FAULTLESS SETTING UP, ALIGNMENT AND STANCE.

HEAD SLIGHTLY TO THE RIGHT

This little tip is very valuable for when you have to play a long shot, for example, a long iron toward a well-protected green. Before starting the backswing, turn your head slightly to the right in order to assist the rotation of your shoulder beneath your chin. Among celebrated players who do this are Jack Nicklaus and Greg Norman.

LOOK TOWARD THE TARGET

How many golfers tense up during the set up, their eyes transfixed on the ball for several seconds … With a resulting slice or thinned shot! If you have this problem, solve it by turning your head toward the target, then the ball, and repeat this several times. This should help you to relax.

LEFT EYE ON THE BALL

A common fault is the inability of many players to keep their left sides behind the ball during the downswing. To correct this, you only need to make a small adjustment when setting up. Concentrate on keeping your left eye on the right half of the ball and try to maintain this line throughout the swing. You will be surprised at the result. Remember – left eye on the right.

THE SPONGE WHICH MOVES MOUNTAINS

To hit the ball hard, the question of weight distribution is of the greatest importance. If you don't transfer the body weight to the left side sufficiently during the downswing, you will never enjoy the feeling of hitting a long ball. If you have poor weight distribution, then a tip is to get two sponges, one thicker than the other, and put them under your right foot. You will then start with 70 percent of the body weight on the right side, and will transfer the weight better during the downswing.

A GLASS PANEL ▲

The plane of your swing depends on your position in relation to the ball. This is affected by your height: if you are tall, the plane will be vertical, and if you are short, it will be flatter. This is what Ben Hogan was demonstrating when he asked a golfer to imagine a panel of glass on his shoulders with his head poking through it. In the backswing, the shoulders turn, rubbing against the inside of the glass. The arms remain parallel to the plane right up to the top of the backswing.

THE IMPORTANCE OF THE MAKE OF BALL

Try this little trick to test whether you are well-aligned. When setting up, place the ball on the tee so that the make of the ball (i.e. its brand name) is visible and aimed at the target. Then keep your feet, hips and shoulders parallel to the name. This is very simple, but very effective.

A CLUB ON THE PELVIS ▶

To check the angle of the chest and to correct alignment of hips and feet, hold a club at the level of your pelvis and lean forward, keeping your legs straight.

GOOD BALL POSITION

The lowest point of the swing arc is under the left shoulder. This is where the ball should be placed for all normal shots. It should never be further in front than the outside of the left shoulder, nor further behind than the left side of the neck.

THE CHALK TEST

If you are concerned about the divots you are taking, check these three essential points before you play: your target, the width of your stance and the ball position. Do not be afraid to draw two horizontal lines in front of you and to place a tee peg in front of each foot. You will benefit from this by seeing the angle of your divots, and discover if their line is inside or outside the target line. As soon as you are in position, move aside and see if you were correct. If not, put it right.

THE HEEL OF THE CLUB ON THE BALL

Many of us have a good backswing, but a mediocre downswing. Main fault: hitting from the top. To avoid this, some of the leading pros, such as Fuzzy Zoeller, recommend positioning the club with its heel just behind the ball when setting up. This makes the backswing more on the inside.

sufficiently equated. For example, if the ball is too far in front or behind, the shoulder alignment will be modified. If it is too far in front, the shoulders will be too "open" and if it is too far behind, the shoulders will be too "closed."

The position of the head during the set up should begin square, so that an imaginary line could be drawn parallel to the target line. At the start of the backswing, it can turn slightly to the right. Alignment is modified every time you want to impart spin on the ball.

Alignment Errors

– Body and club aligned to the right: the most common error. With an outside-to-inside downswing, you are liable to slice.
– Body aligned to the right of the target, club aligned to the left: certainly no hook, but no length either.
– Body aligned to the left, clubface to the right: an error made by many good players. You can achieve a fade if you hit through well. But you can also hit a hook, or, even worse, a pull, if your backswing is too much on the inside.
– Body and club to the left: the club rises on the outside. You will be locked, and your shot will lack length and accuracy.

Work on your "Routine"

To achieve an automatic playing posture, always follow the same routine:
– align the club face with the target, after checking the line of flight by stepping back from the ball. Choose an intermediate target and use a vertical line going through the club;
– assume your stance and align your body;
– after aligning club and body, insure that your eyes are also aligned. Lower your head and return it to its original position. Above all, do not pivot sideways;
– keeping the same posture, distribute the weight of the club depending on which one you are using.

According to Jack Nicklaus, "posture is quite simply the most important thing in golf." Johnny Miller used the image of the gun: "Once you are in position, you only have to pull the trigger." It is interesting to note just how crucial posture and alignment are regarded by the great players; perhaps they are viewed as being even more significant than the swing itself. By contrast, amateur players often neglect this aspect of the game, and they do so at their peril. Let's hope that this analysis will inspire you to think about it more carefully!

ALIGN YOURSELF TWICE

A lot of golfers position themselves poorly when setting up.

Feet and shoulders in particular are not aimed at the target, and the clubface is too far to the right. A push, a pull or a slice can result. To align yourself properly, follow this sequence: 1. position the club just behind the ball, perpendicular in relation to the target; 2. step back a little from your normal stance. This should enable you to follow through along the target line, instead of cutting across it.

ALIGN YOURSELF ON TILES

If you have a tiled floor take a club and try to align yourself correctly. The tips of the toes on one of the rows of tiles represents body alignment. The clubface is at a right angle to the line (the tiles) representing the target line. Practice until you feel completely at ease.

IMAGINE A LINE STRETCHING TO THE TARGET

How many shots go wrong due to bad alignment! Pull, slice, push etc. There is often no need to look any further for the reason for a bad shot. Take your time, before setting up, look at the target from behind the ball and visualize a line going from the ball to the target. Once in position, all you need to do is to think of following through along this line.

THE CLUB AS A GUIDE ▶

If you have attended any championships, you will have noticed that even great players like Jack Nicklaus and Tom Watson occasionally lay a club alongside them on the ground when practicing. Why? For correct alignment. Imagine that the target is a long way away; another club aimed at the target allows the clubface, feet, hips and shoulders to be better aligned.

THE WAGGLE
AND THE TAKEAWAY

The waggle movement used by the champions

Although it is not the most fundamental aspect of the swing, or really even part of it, the waggle can be of great use. Jack Nicklaus has always effected a slight wrist movement and waggling is also a characteristic of Nick Faldo's game.

What is a Waggle?

The waggle is the movement or movements which precede the start of the swing itself. It relaxes the player particularly when using the driver, it gives a good trajectory to the start of the backswing and prepares the hand action better. The waggle should not be viewed as a gimmick – it is used in serious play. It is a miniature copy of the actual swing. There is no sense in waggling if you are going to cock your wrists immediately you start the backswing, as this is contrary to how the actual swing should be. Preparation for the swing is similar to the checks you make before moving off in your car.

Of course, you can always start a car without making any checks at all, but this is not advisable. In golf, it's the waggle that starts the engine.

A PERFECT EXAMPLE OF
THE CLASSIC TAKEAWAY:
THE ALL-IN-ONE
BACKSWING OF THE
AUSTRALIAN GREG
NORMAN. HIS TAKEAWAY
IS FUNDAMENTAL TO THE
REST OF HIS SWING.

Golf is a very individual sport, and so is the waggle. It has no precise rules. Some people raise their club once, others do it several times. The waggle can also be a backswing, downswing and even a follow through, in short it is anything of a preparatory nature, but it is not fixed and stereotyped. A lot of players try to develop a waggle, but without success. It is not a question of changing your grip ten times before the backswing. Nor is it a case of adopting a more comfortable position to the detriment of a good swing. The aim is to try and relax, while sticking to the correct principles. But even these are variable in such a personal area of the game.

The waggle is particularly useful when playing a shot with spin, a hook or a slice. For a hook or draw, players should absorb and memorize the type of movement they are going to make. They should therefore use a waggle which will include starting the backswing on the inside, or the opposite if they wish to make a sliced shot.

It must be emphasized that the waggle is not vital, but can be extremely useful, especially if a player tenses up.

If this applies to you, try it and see the difference!

The takeaway

The takeaway is of prime importance to the rest of the swing, yet three quarters of golfers do not know the real meaning of the term. Just as the first three months after conception are vital to a child's life, so a poor takeaway can be disastrous to a golf swing.

The term "takeaway" applies to the first twenty inches (50 cm) of the backswing. Virtually everything depends on it – the swing plane is determined at this point, the swing arc is formed, rhythm and tempo are under way. Let's go over the different points involved.

In the classic takeaway – and there are different schools of thought on this – the club is an extension of the ball as it moves away, the club face remaining square. You must realize that this is theoretical, in so far as the distance in relation to the ball modifies the data. If you are closer than normal to the ball, the club will tend to remain an extension of the ball for longer.

On the other hand, if you are further away from the ball, the club will quickly move to the inside.

THE GOLF COURSE AT MANDELIEU, NEAR CANNES, IS ONE OF THE MOST POPULAR IN FRANCE. IT HAS AN INTERNATIONAL CLIENTELE AND IS A MARVELOUS HOLIDAY COURSE.

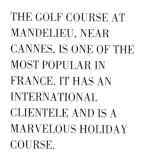

FRENCH
PROFESSIONAL, MARC-
ANTOINE FARRY
DEMONSTRATES A
TEXTBOOK SET UP,
ALIGNMENT AND
STANCE.

Make Sure you are Square!

It is very important for the club face to remain square – perpendicular – in relation to the target line. It is the best way to insure that the club is in a good position at the top of the backswing. If the face is open or closed at the takeaway, you will need to compensate somewhere to re-establish the balance.

This is never a good idea. An effective way of checking if the clubface is square is to see if the end of the club is pointing skywards.

The Role of the Wrists

Some people believe that the hands, arms and shoulders should act as an extension of each other, without cocking the wrists. This is the classic school. Then there are those who believe that since the left hand dominates the swing, the right hand has to be cocked. The angle formed by the left arm and the club resulting from the

cocking of the wrists should give more power to the swing. This early assumption of angle is carried out using the top three fingers of the left hand when the arms rise behind the ball.

Adherents to this theory believe that the club acquires a good plane more quickly. Also, this angle causes the ball to be struck late.

Mind you, everyone agrees that the backswing is not initiated by the arms alone.

Four Check Points

– The left wrist should form a 90 degree angle with the left arm, acting as a reinforcement. Check this when the wrist is at waist height.
– The clubhead should be slightly open.
– Body weight is slightly to the right.
– The club should move slowly, close to the ground and inside the target line – but not too much, or you will get too much spin on the ball.

A GOOD TAKEAWAY

At the takeaway, the left hand should be leading: hold the club with three fingers of the left hand and remove the thumb and index finger of the right hand from the shaft. Then take the club away from the ball with the feeling of stretching the left arm.

THE CLUB AND THE NAVEL

In order to swing the hips and keep the club close to the ground without bending the wrists too soon, you can carry out a simple test by checking whether the club shaft is still lined up with an extension of

your navel, which will move during the backswing.

USE TEES FOR A GOOD SWING PLANE

Put a ball on a tee. Then put in two other tees next to each other, about four or five inches (10–12 cm) in front of the ball to the right. Do the same thing again with two other tees, this time in front and to the left of the ball. This layout will provide marker points to check whether your swing plane is correct, and not too outside or too inside.

If the club touches the tees

on the right during the backswing, your plane is poor because it is too much on the outside. If you hit one of the tees in the ground on the downswing, then again, your club is too much on the outside. The correct plane avoids all the tees, except, of course, the one on which the ball is sitting.

USE A TEE TO KEEP CLOSE TO THE GROUND

If you raise your club too quickly because your right hand is too strong, put in a tee about 12 inches (30 cm) from the ball,

just inside the line of flight. Normally you should be able to hear the sound of the driver clipping the tee at the takeaway.

MIME THE FOLLOW THROUGH

To memorize how to execute the downswing, pretend you are following through on impact, with the club about 20 inches (50 cm) in front of the ball. This preliminary swing is much more effective than the traditional "forward press" where only the hands move ahead in relation to the ball.

THE BACKSWING

No end of golfers try very hard to improve their downswing, when their backswing is far from perfect.

However, it is very rare to see a good player with a bad backswing. What are we aiming for with a good backswing? Essentially, to store up the maximum amount of energy, which will be released in the downswing to obtain greater length. How is it done? Once again, there are several theories, which are basically similar, but vary slightly in terms of form.

Backswing with the Top of the Body only
This has the advantage of making the movement more compact. It is not an obvious movement because it requires great flexibility. Conversely, it seems a pity not to use the lower half of the body.

The disadvantage of this method is that weight transfer may not take place or takes place under worse conditions, which may produce problems in the downswing.

Backswing with the Top of the Body First
The top of the body leads initially, then the left side is activated. This method has the advantage of adhering to the priorities without eliminating one part of the body for the benefit of another.

All Together
The shoulders, arms, hands, hips, and club all rise at the same time. The advantage: an easier movement and greater rotation. It is

THE AMERICAN LARRY NELSON PROVIDES A GOOD EXAMPLE OF A PLAYER WITH A SOLID BACKSWING, SHOWING A FIRM RIGHT LEG, A WELL EXTENDED LEFT ARM WITH HIS HEAD POSITIONED DIRECTLY OVER THE LEFT SHOULDER.

recommended for players of medium to heavy build or those lacking suppleness. Club-body coordination at the start of the swing definitely helps the rest of the swing. The great Jack Nicklaus insisted on a slow and very deliberate start to the backswing. If you put everything into the start, you risk accelerating the swing and ending up with too fast a swing. The reverse can be equally bad. If the backswing is too slow, often the downswing is too hurried.

Widen the Circle

The golfer who bends the left arm a little during the backswing is often advised by colleagues to insure that the left arm is kept straight. It is an excellent piece of advice, but what is the reason for it? It is because the right side dominates throughout the backswing. If you try to "widen the circle" with the clubhead, there is more chance of making the left side work, and thus of keeping the left arm straight.

We might ask the question "What is it that creates power?" Principally, there are two factors involved – one is turning, the other is leverage. To reach a par 4 hole in two shots, especially if it is a long hole, it is important to create a tension between the upper and lower halves of the body during the

backswing. But to create this tension you need to be in good physical condition, which is unfortunately not the case with everyone. Particularly if you spend the whole week sitting in an office.

Jack Nicklaus describes the main role of the lower half of the body in his book, *Golf, my way*. It provides, he suggests, a stable base while creating some resistance to the action of the top half of the body. The latter directs the movement, and the lower half follows. This is exactly the chain reaction discussed above.

Most people know that you need to pivot in order to hit the ball any distance, but few people know why. The answer is quite simple. Just for fun, try to hit the ball with your hands and arms, without turning your shoulders. The result cannot be anything but mediocre or bad. If you pivot, the clubhead is fairly flat upon impact, enabling the ball to be hit cleanly. If you don't pivot, the angle of attack will be vertical, the ball might be topped, and will have no length in any case.

The second good reason for pivoting is because of the power it generates. When you hit a good drive it is largely because the pivot was good. However, there should never be a conscious effort to rotate the shoulders.

Although you can't expect to play well by

THE GOLF COURSE AT FIRETHORN, OMAHA, DESIGNED BY PERRY DYE, ONE OF THE TWO SONS OF PETE DYE. THE SPIRIT OF THE DYE FAMILY IS PRESERVED HERE ON THIS COURSE NOTED FOR ITS GREAT TECHNICAL DIFFICULTY.

PLAYING TECHNIQUE

There is one crucial thing you must think about at the start of the backswing: the clubface must remain square from start to finish. It can only be square at the finish if it is square at the beginning. You have to act quickly. How? By starting the swing with the left hand and arm. The hands should not turn but should remain passive. They will act later.

PIVOT IN A BARREL

The main purpose of pivoting is to create power. Energy is stored by virtue of the action of the lower half of the body up to the hips. A common piece of advice is to create a mental image of a barrel surrounding the body from the ground to the navel, just large enough to enable the hip action to develop. This is because the hips create the pivot, together with the shoulder action, which activates the arms and the hands. On the downswing, the barrel will "explode" due to the lateral hip action.

HIPS FIRST

After checking that your set up position is correct, think about turning your hips before anything else, and of lifting the left heel toward the ball. After this, you only have to lift the club and your weight is already practically transferred to the right side.

SOFT GRIP ON THE BACKSWING

A very pronounced right-hand action should not be used during the takeaway. A good way of avoiding this is to hold the club with only the top three fingers of the left hand, and the middle and ring fingers of the right hand. In other words, the thumb and index finger of the right hand should not touch the club shaft.

This is to enable you to stay closer to the ground during the takeaway, the critical moment which starts off the backswing.

TO IMPROVE ROTATION

Various conditions have to be fulfilled in order to achieve greater distance. Two of these are especially important: good rotation and good weight transfer. To improve these two areas, adopt a wider stance than usual for the drive, keep your hands by your sides, turn your head and the top half of your body alternately to the right and left. Try to look over your shoulder. Do this several times. Regular practice should eliminate any problems you might have with the pivot.

A CLUB BEHIND THE BACK ▶

When practicing, good players often use this technique to warm up. The exercise is simple and effective, and consists of putting a club behind one's back and pivoting to the right and then left. It should feel as if the club is lying horizontally.

SHOULDER UNDER THE CHIN ▶

The following tip is only a case of applying basic principles: for a better pivot, turn the knee inward during the backswing and bring the left shoulder under the chin, until the knee and chin form a line pointing just behind the ball.

THE BACKSWING

THE HIPS

You must turn your hips during the backswing. To help explain this idea, picture this: at the top of the backswing, the right back pocket of your trousers should be just above your right heel.

LIFT THE LEFT HEEL

With the exception of approach shots, the left foot should always be raised inward during the backswing; it increases pivot. Be careful! Raise it to the inside and not the outside, or the pivot will be non-existent.

SWING WITHOUT THE CLUB ▶

In the address position, pretend you have a club in your hand. Keep your left hand in position and put your right hand behind your back. Lift your left hand until it goes past the right shoulder, then have a club held up for you by a friend parallel to the target.

THE RIGHT SHOULDER

To improve your rotation, instead of thinking automatically about your left shoulder, think of the action of the right one. You will increase your chances of hitting the ball a long way.

PAUSE AT THE TOP

If you watch the great players, you will notice that some of them pause at the top of the backswing. This prevents the downswing from being too hurried, and allows the sequence to happen in order. Think about this – put a stool behind you and touch it with your right side at the top of the backswing. Pausing at the top of the backswing also enables the left hand to stop the action of the right hand, which tends to dominate at the start of the downswing.

relying on the shoulders alone, the opposite is equally true. The shoulder action should never overshadow the arm action. The club is raised by virtue of the arm action, and the left side follows naturally. All the same, you mustn't forget that the left arm is connected to the shoulder!

It is often said that the downswing is effected out in the same way as the backswing. Well, the shoulders play an important part in the backswing, but it is not advisable for them to do the same in the downswing. It is a question of priority and harmony, and it is important to avoid too pronounced a shoulder action, which will produce a potentially inside-to-outside downswing, or the reverse. Neither of these is desirable. Also, it is vital for the hips to turn more than the shoulders, as they will take the whole of the lower part of the body with them.

The action of the lower half of the body

This consists of several things. Initially, it is concerned with the transfer of weight from left to right: this is automatic and progressive, and the right leg should lock and resist pressure, so that the swing axis does not change. The leg position should not alter drastically, rather it becomes very slightly flexed.

In harmony with this action, the left leg relaxes and turns inward to assist in achieving the weight shift. Many golfers raise their left foot and turn it to the outside, which only makes the transfer more tricky.

At the top of the backswing, the weight of the body is on the right side, the hips and shoulders have turned, the club is in the correct swing plane, being neither too flat nor too vertical. Everything is ready. Yet a lot of people prefer to pause for a second or two before commencing the downswing. This imperceptible pause allows time to check that the machine is ready to work. It is not vital, but it has its use ...

To sum up:
– Action of the top half of the body: hips and shoulders turn.
– The left arm directs the swing and takes the left side with it.
– The lower part of the body follows: transfer of weight to the right side, left heel raised.
– At the top of the backswing, the club is parallel to the line of the swing plane and the swing plane is neither too flat nor too vertical.

CLOSE-UP OF A FAULTLESS ROTATION OF THE UPPER BODY, COURTESY OF THE 1984 MASTERS CHAMPION, BEN CRENSHAW.

THUMBS UNDER

You can check that your alignment is correct by looking at your thumbs at the top of the backswing. If they are both well wedged under the shaft of the club, this means that the club is in line in relation to the target. If not, you must correct it; a good downswing depends on it.

PUT A BALL UNDER YOUR RIGHT ARM

To check if the pivot is good, put a ball under your right arm. If it drops out during the backswing, it is likely that the pivot has not been executed correctly.

NO. 1 FRIEND

If you are convinced that the only way you are going to make any progress is to have good rotation of the hips and shoulders, then ask a friend to assist you. For example, ask them to stand behind you and help you to turn your hips using their hands. Do it several times, then try to recall the feeling when you are on your own.

A PIECE OF STRING UNDER THE LEFT KNEE

If your swing lacks aggression, and you think this is due to your failure to transfer your weight sufficiently during the backswing, imagine you have a piece of string tied from your right hip to your left knee. If you pivot well, the string will pull the left knee back in the opposite direction to the target.

THE SPRING ▶

Think of your spine as a spring in order to improve the way you turn your upper body. During the backswing, keep your head still and put your left shoulder under your chin. The idea of a spring will then become clear to you. In the downswing, the spring will uncoil normally.

THE DOWNSWING

If someone told you that by the time you begin your downswing, "It's all over bar the shouting," would you believe them? If we think of the golf swing as a sequence, this clearly means that one is committed, or almost, before the downswing begins, and it follows that if the backswing is good, the downswing has every chance of being a success. If the backswing is poor, then you just might be able to compensate for it on the downswing, but it is never a good idea to tamper with your swing. The downswing takes place so quickly, in barely a second. Everything therefore takes on disproportionate importance. At impact, the relative weight of the driver head is more than a ton, and its speed is over 125 m.p.h. (200 km/h). Astounding, isn't it?

In order to have any hope of developing a good downswing, at least three criteria have to be fulfilled: generation of maximum clubhead speed; the tracing of a line close to the line of flight with the clubhead at impact and immediately thereafter, and a clubhead that is kept pointing at the target for as long as possible.

The golfer who achieves these three requirements can hope to hit a good shot. The action of the clubhead should be one of traction rather than a push. This is only possible if the hand, arm and left side control the swing. It is

THE GREAT NANCY
LOPEZ, ONE OF THE MOST
BRILLIANT PERFORMERS
IN WOMEN'S GOLF.
THE PHOTOGRAPH
ILLUSTRATES A GOOD
DOWNSWING, ONE WHICH
COMBINES
EFFECTIVENESS AND
GRACE.

GERMANY'S BERNHARD
LANGER HAS ONE OF
THE BEST SWINGS IN
THE WORLD, AS WELL
AS ONE OF THE MOST
CONSISTENT.

only when the right side dominates that the clubhead action turns into a push. Generating maximum speed with the clubhead depends greatly on the quality of the backswing. The backswing serves to lift the club so that at the top of the swing there is sufficient speed to launch the downswing and hit the ball with power. It's the same action as a butcher uses, when he creates power by lifting his cleaver. In a complete swing, the wrists cock automatically at the moment when the club begins its downswing. In fact – and this is very important – the clubhead reaches the top of the backswing when the downswing has already begun.

During the backswing, when the hands are at shoulder height, the clubhead has already started to come down. The wrists will cock automatically.

To avoid those errors that we shall explore, it is important to understand that the left side should dominate, as it does in the backswing. The lower half of the body turns to the left in the direction of the target, then the hips, hands, arms, wrists, and club all follow, in a complete single movement.

To get the clubface square at impact, which is the number one aim with a golf swing, don't forget the principles already explained – each will help. The problem is that during the swing it is

practically impossible to exert even the slightest control over the clubhead. Also, before you even start the swing, it is a good idea to simulate the decisive action of the downswing mentally.

If you tend to slice the ball, my advice is to try to bring the left forearm toward the right one when hitting. Another idea is to think of the toe of the club as being ahead of the heel in the impact zone. Even if you cannot actually do this, the act of trying will help to correct some of the slice. Looking at your swing in a mirror is equally instructive. In the backswing, the right arm bends and the left is straight, while the reverse happens during the downswing, the left arm bends slightly when the right is straight.

Beginners and even average players do not bend their right arm enough in the backswing, nor the left arm in the downswing. There is definitely better control of the swing and the follow-through is better if the right elbow is close to the body during the backswing and the left elbow is close to the body in the downswing.

Let's think about the follow-through. A famous quote states that: "The ball is merely accidental to the club's trajectory." This suggests that the swing is not finished when the ball has been hit. There is still the vital follow-through to consider.

RIGHT SHOULDER ▶
UNDERNEATH

Even though to effect this is difficult, because the action takes place in the minimum amount of time, it is important to practice the shoulder movement for the downswing. The right shoulder should pass under the chin. In this way, the head will remain still during most of the swing. If the right shoulder is raised, then the head will turn toward the target too soon and the downswing plane will almost certainly be outside-to-inside, inevitably producing a slice.

HANDS IN FRONT

This tip can be both useful and dangerous if taken literally. The ideal position for the hands upon impact is in front of the ball. By virtue of this, the shot will have more power. A forward hand position starts from the backswing, with the legs building up momentum at the start of the downswing, and the wrists held back. If the hands are in front, the ball will be whipped up better. If they are behind, there will be less power.

ON ONE LEG ▶

Have you ever tried hitting the ball standing on one leg? It's difficult to begin with, but when you stand on two feet again, it's all much easier. There is no need to lift the club higher than the hips. Try it with a short iron, and if you lack confidence, shadow the swing first without the ball. A more sophisticated version is to address the ball, raise the left leg, lift the club, remain on the right leg then put the left leg back down in the same place. Try the exercise without the ball to improve synchronization.

At this moment, the arms are both fully extended. At impact, a golfer's balance is precarious, hence the risk of error is increased. On the other hand, after impact, during the follow-through, the body is perfectly straight, even compact. Work on the follow-through to improve your weak points.

Why accelerate at impact?

The secret of a good follow-through lies in the acceleration of the clubhead. The greater the speed of the club at this moment, the further the ball will go. But – and this is a common question – why accelerate after impact when the ball is already on its way? Good question! It is simply because if the club does not accelerate after impact, then it must have lost speed before impact, which is serious. All coaches will tell you that no-one actually decides to accelerate at the moment of impact. This operation is initiated right from the beginning, with acceleration commencing at the start of the downswing. It's all a question of drive! Beginners tend to think you need to be about seven feet tall (2 m) and weigh 250 pounds (113 kg) to be able to hit the ball hard. But it's more a question of coordination and timing than of muscle.

PLAY EARTH-BALL ▶

To learn how to play earth-ball, try this little exercise: place two balls on top of each other with a bit of earth to cement them together. The exercise consists of hitting the bottom ball first. If you do this, you will notice that the lower ball will follow the direction of the target, and will rise relatively little, while the top ball will rise into the air very quickly.

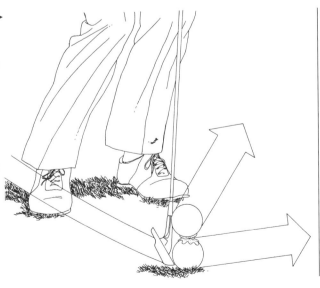

TO CHECK THE CLUB FACE

Here is an easy way to find out if the club face is square (perpendicular to the target line), open or closed at impact: after impact and follow-through, when the club is at waist height, look at the club face. If it is pointing to the left, the face is closed, and if it is pointing to the right, it is open. If the face is pointing straight upwards, it is square.

SHAKE HANDS

To achieve the correct feel during the backswing and particularly in the follow-through, imagine you are shaking a friend's hand. This idea should enable you to extend your arms out straight and enlarge the swing arc at the same time.

OFF TARGET

If you are not playing straight, it is perhaps because the palm of your right hand is not square in relation to the target line upon impact.

THE PEBBLE ▶

Instead of balancing the club on the ball with your hands, try to bring the right shoulder under during the downswing. When the right elbow almost touches the right hip, turn your right hand under as if you were throwing a pebble into the sea. The follow-through movement will become more natural.

RING THE BELL

Although it's not necessary to have all these mental images in your head when you are playing, there must be at least one which is particularly suited to your situation. For example, a lot of players have a weak left side on the downswing and a poor wrist action. To eliminate this problem, address the ball and adopt your usual grip. Then put your right hand behind your back and bring down the left hand only, as if you were ringing a bell. Start with a small club and increase the difficulty progressively.

TIED TO THE STAKE

It is important not to sway the top part of the body if you want to hit or throw an object successfully. Even good players "forget" this principle and move the top half of their body during the downswing. To counteract this error, pretend that the top of your body, around the chest, is tied to a post. This has the advantage of eliminating sway. Take care! this tip is not for everyone, particularly not for beginners, as it could be the start of bad weight transfer. But it's excellent for the more experienced player.

THE SPANIARD JOSE
MARIA OLAZABAL,
SHOWN HERE IN SOME
DIFFICULTY, WITH A
WOOD ON HIS RIGHT.
THE EFFECTIVENESS
OF HIS DOWNSWING
SHOULD ENABLE HIM
TO BYPASS THIS
OBSTACLE WITHOUT
ANY PROBLEM.

Coordination and impulsion, are the two key words for success. Good coordination implies a good head position, not completely still but turning on an axis which goes round the back of the neck. At the moment of impact, centrifugal force automatically causes the head to move backward. This may seem to be a mere detail, but it's much more than that. Golfers with their heads in front have a dominant right side in the backswing, which will have serious consequences: the downswing will start badly, with a too pronounced shoulder action.

In order to appreciate this negative aspect, remember that one of the aims of the backswing is to store up the maximum amount of energy by combining full shoulder rotation with a less pronounced pivot of the hips. This premature shoulder action decreases the energy produced, and therefore reduces clubhead speed.

Another common error: the head is raised, due frequently to the left arm collapsing upon impact. The weight of this impact is in the order of 66 to 88 pounds (30–40 kg), which is considerable, and the body registers the impact, especially in the case of a bad shot. To achieve the vital extension of the left arm, think of pushing it down and outward and not toward the target upon impact.

There are at least five key principles to remember with regard to the downswing:
– the head should only move back very slightly upon impact. People who move their heads to the left during the downswing often hit slices, pushes, hooks (see following chapters).
– The left arm should be more or less straight, as an extension of the left shoulder. The hands should be slightly in front of the ball upon impact, with the left shoulder higher than the right one. This is the best method of insuring that the clubhead follows the target line and that the body weight transfers to the left.
– The transfer of body weight takes place from right to left.
– Above all, the lower half of the body initiates the downswing before the top half, but with an unhurried hip movement.
– In the follow-through, the toe of the club points skyward and the back of the right hand is directed at the target.

BALL IN THE CENTER

A good way of checking that your first shot has gone straight is to look at the tee. Concentrate on watching it after impact. If you notice any movement in it, you can be sure that you were well aligned in relation to the ball.

ELBOWS ATTACHED

In order to keep your arms close to the body upon impact, which is vital for a compact swing, make sure that your right elbow is close to your right side at the start of the backswing and the left elbow is close to the left side during the follow-through, i.e. just after impact. All this will help to improve the ball's trajectory, and give better control and more power. What a lot of plus points!

RIGHT HIP FORWARD

How many times does this happen: a very quick backswing, then a downswing which starts with the upper body? An eternal refrain! Result: the head of the club meets the ball on the outside, and there is scarcely anything to choose between a pull or a slice. To avoid this mistake, it is vital for the upper body to keep behind the ball upon impact. In concrete terms, this means that your right hip should be in front in relation to your chin. This will also make you keep your head still.

HOLDING THE CLUB BACK

To generate clubhead speed, you need to hold the club back in relation to the body. It is much harder to achieve in practice than to describe. Address the ball with your normal stance and grip. Then lift the left hand from the club and raise the right hand to shoulder level. Place the left hand lower on the shaft than the right one. Practice this continuously, keeping within the shoulder-waist area. The action of the left hand aims to prevent the wrists from cocking too quickly and stop the hands from moving first.

REDUCE THE GAP

People often think they only need to use their hands and arms to hit the ball. Wrong. One of the best methods is to use the lower part of the body, and more accurately, to reduce the gap between the legs during the downswing. The right knee should move toward the left knee, without causing a rupture, of course!

THE FINISH

It can never be said too often that since the golf swing is a sequence, the finish is only a consequence of what has gone before. Very few good players, however, have a poor finish, and many average players or beginners have, shall we say, a fairly unorthodox one. "Show me your finish and I'll tell you how good you are." Yes, the finish is important. It all depends on knowing which finish to adopt. Are there several types of finish or is there only one which is the right one?

In broad terms, there are two kinds of finish. The first, or so-called classic finish, is characterized by the hands finishing high, behind the head, with the club behind. Another identifying factor is that the left arm remains extended for as long as possible, directed toward the target line.

Arnold Palmer championed this type of high finish, and it was imitated by Severiano Ballesteros on many occasions during his early years. Unfortunately, not everyone is a Palmer or a Ballesteros!

Golfers with this kind of finish are, in fact, often restricted, due to excessive action of the body,

THE KING OF GOLF: JACK
NICKLAUS HAS WON
TWENTY MAJOR TITLES
DURING AN
EXCEPTIONAL CAREER.

JEAN VAN DE VELDE,
ONE OF THE MOST
ACCOMPLISHED
FRENCH PLAYERS AND
A WINNER ON THE PGA
EUROPEAN TOUR.

mainly the shoulders and hips, which prevents the clubhead from moving in the correct line.

The second type of finish, adopted by numerous latter-day champions, is a flatter, more circular finish.

What are the differences? The chief difference lies in the fact that with this type of finish, the hands and arms are used more in order to generate clubhead speed. There is also less call on the body overall to make the clubface square upon impact. Result: in the downswing, the club "travels" longer inside the line of flight, and the hands and wrists cock more quickly. Above all, and this is visible and obvious, the left arm bends immediately after impact to create a good follow-through. This type of finish is assisted by a slightly stronger grip, with the left hand turned more to the right.

Which is better? It varies. You don't choose the finish you have – it depends on the individual swing. The golfer with a vertical or upright swing stands a good chance of having a finish like Palmer. On the other hand, a flatter swing will probably lead to a rounder, more encircling finish with the arms and hands well behind and parallel to the ground.

A REAR VIEW OF THE LEADING IRISH PLAYER, RONAN RAFFERTY, EUROPEAN NUMBER ONE IN 1989. HE HAS AN EXCELLENT, COMPACT AND WELL-BALANCED FINISH.

PHOTO FINISH

In golf, one of the key words is balance. Otherwise, it's no go! One way of checking whether your swing is balanced is to look at your finish. If it is awkward and unstable, it's because you have hit too hard, too quickly. To correct this, try to slow down your swing, and follow-through well after impact. By doing this you should be able to remain in the finish position for at least five seconds without any difficulty – a test which should not be neglected.

BREAK THE TAPE AT THE FINISH LINE

The average player often forgets to transfer his weight to the left side during the downswing. To get this idea of transfer ingrained in your mind, imagine you are a winning athlete crossing the finishing line and breaking the tape. In this case you are breaking it with your waist, the part of the body which is in front of the rest.

LIKE THE PROS

If you watch the great players, you will notice that the majority never finish their swing without taking the club to waist height, with the face pointing skyward. They hold this for a few seconds. Reason for this: a more flowing swing and a better plane.

LIFT YOUR RIGHT FOOT

In the same way that you should raise your left heel during the backswing, it is also advisable to lift your right foot at the finish. This proves that weight transfer has taken place correctly during the downswing and shows good body balance after impact. The right knee should be close to the left one. Don't be tempted to lift your foot after the swing is finished. It won't help at all.

You should be able to lift your right foot to the level of the left knee. Can you?

TEMPO AND SPIN

The major role of tempo

Can an analogy be drawn between the golf swing and a piece of classical music? Only those who play neither golf nor music could fail to see it. Basic technique apart, all the rest is no more than a matter of rhythm, tempo and timing. *In Golf, my way*, Jack Nicklaus defines these three essential terms: "Tempo indicates the overall pace of the swing, its speed, the time elapsing between the backswing and the end of the follow-through.

Rhythm describes the variations in speed within the general pace, and timing expresses the way in which the movements form a sequence. It's the result of the marriage between pace (tempo) and fluidity (rhythm)."

There are few sports where tempo plays as prominent a role as it does in golf. For example, in tennis, with the exception of the service, the movements are made comparatively suddenly, even if touch and rhythm play their part. Golf is not a reflex game, but a reflective game. It is important not to rush things, to take one's time so insuring that the different movements are coordinated in the best possible sequence. Correct tempo is the guarantee that everything is working properly. It is important to point out at this stage in our analysis that if the rhythm is bad,

PRACTICE MAKES
PERFECT: THE SOUTH
AFRICAN GARY PLAYER,
ONE OF THE GAME'S
TRUE LEGENDS.
GOLF IS PRIMARILY A
GAME IN WHICH RHYTHM
IS OF PARAMOUNT
IMPORTANCE.

the shot has every chance of being bad, even if the fundamental principles of the swing are adhered to. On the other hand, good rhythm can salvage many shots.

It is not easy to find one's own rhythm. That is why, once this has been achieved, everything possible should be done to preserve it. Unfortunately, in golf, rhythm varies according to the shot. There is a great difference between a lobbed wedge shot and a powerful drive.

The hands are the main obstacle to achieving good tempo. It is almost impossible to play predominantly with the hands and have good tempo. Excessive hand action prevents it. The players with the best tempo are those who use their hands the least during the swing. They also have a slower swing.

Is it necessary to be slow in order to have good tempo? Yes and no. Those who were ever lucky enough to watch Sam Snead in his prime will never forget the lessons in tempo he gave each time he played. His swing was always identical, even if his tempo varied according to the shot he had to play. The start of his backswing was relatively quick, slowing before the top, and it accelerated progressively as it returned toward the ball.

In contrast, starting slowly then accelerating in the middle of the backswing before slowing down is not wise. Golfers who have a rhythm problem are advised to rest their club on the ground when setting up. This prevents their having to lift it too quickly at the start of the backswing.

Although tempo is largely related to temperament, it is obvious that every swing has its own tempo. The nervous, aggressive player will have a quick tempo, while the more phlegmatic golfer will have a slower tempo. That's the nature of things. But it is also undeniable that the golfer with a wide swing arc and lots of lift, who hits the ball coming down, will have a slower tempo than a player with a shorter swing, with reduced lift. This type of player will adopt a quicker tempo in order to generate sufficient speed at impact. This can be reversed, by saying that the quicker the swing, the more compact it should be. The slower it is, the wider it is.

In order to develop a suitable tempo and consistent rhythm, it is important to complete the backswing properly. This is especially relevant when you are under pressure, when circumstances are unfavorable, for example when the weather is bad or when there is a difficult shot to play. We have all experienced such

FEEL THE SPEED OF YOUR SWING

To gain a feel for the speed of your swing, line up three balls on a tee and play them one after the other using a 7 iron. Hit the first ball softly about a third of the normal distance. Hit the second ball harder. Hit the third like a normal shot. Pay attention to finishing the swing and to keeping your balance.

THE HANDKERCHIEF TEST

To find out if your rhythm is good, and if you are achieving appropriate clubhead speed, practice swinging with your eyes closed, or even better, blindfolded with a handkerchief.

TEST SWINGS WITHOUT THE CLUB

A good way of checking that your swing is not too fast is to make several practice swings without a club. Sometimes you will do this naturally without actually knowing why. Don't forget, however, to put a ball in position. You will see that it is the arms which control the shoulders and not the other way round.

A GOOD WARM-UP

Unfortunately it often happens that players arrive with only a few minutes to spare before a competition. There is not enough time for an in-depth practice session. To warm up rapidly, swing with two clubs in your hand (4 and 5 irons for example) for two or three minutes. This will be enough to make your initial shot easier. Even the driver will feel lighter and easier to use.

circumstances.

Completing the backswing means insuring that your left shoulder passes under your chin, and you should have your hands above your head before starting the downswing. If your swing is short, it is important to turn the hips.

Here are some principles which should not be forgotten:
— Good tempo consists in starting the backswing quite slowly, guiding it to the top, and then accelerating on the downswing.
— Tempo depends to a large extent on individual temperament.
— Tempo varies in relation to the nature of the swing.
— Don't accelerate when using a long iron or a wood.

Spin

Why didn't the French champion Jean Garailde become a great world champion at all levels? No doubt there were various reasons; one of which was undoubtedly his inability to master spin. One day, the great Nicklaus was in Paris for a demonstration, and was amazed to discover that the French number one golfer at that time did not

WHY DOES MICHEL TAPIA FIGURE IN THIS GALLERY OF CHAMPIONS? BECAUSE THIS FRENCHMAN HAS ALWAYS BEEN ACKNOWLEDGED AS HAVING ONE OF THE BEST TEMPOS IN EUROPE. EVEN SEVERIANO BALLESTEROS AGREES!

FADE OR DRAW – IT'S
YOUR CHOICE. ONE
THING IS DEFINITE,
THE TECHNIQUE
DIFFERS DEPENDING
ON WHETHER YOU ARE
MAKING A SHOT WITH
LEFT OR RIGHT SPIN.

know how to impart spin on the ball. To be able to send the ball in the same direction repeatedly is good, but to adapt to all situations by maneuvering the ball is even better. Shaping shots, for instance to avoid hazards, is part of the sport, and one of golf's great attractions is having to diversify one's game. It is also one of its difficulties, as there is a narrow line between a successfully shaped shot – a draw – and its failure in the form of a hook, or between a fade and a slice.

Fade

It is much more natural to play a fade than a draw. The fade is a shot whose trajectory starts off on the left then goes to the right. The potential benefit in this kind of shot? Imagine a par 4 hole which doglegs to the right. If you are successful with your fade from the tee, your second shot will be a shorter approach. To play a fade, position your shoulders and feet to the left of the target, open the club face and use your normal swing. The more you want to accentuate this trajectory, the more you accentuate the different positions. It's easy, isn't it? When you practice you will notice that it is easier to play a fade with a long iron than with a short iron, since the clubface is

less open. This means that to avoid a hazard situated to the right for example, you will need to position yourself further to the left than normal, and use a long iron. Take care: this swing tends to slice the ball and decrease its length. It's a good idea to take one more club than is usually required for the distance.

The Draw

If you are an accurate player seeking greater length, the draw will help you. The ball which is drawn traditionally travels further, especially when the wind is favorable.

To make this shot, you do the reverse of the fade. Align your feet and shoulders to the right of the target, or parallel with the trajectory you wish the ball to follow. The clubface is closed at address, which will impart spin on to the ball and make it roll further.

One condition is necessary for a draw to be successful: the body must not move, the hands control everything. If the body moves, the hands get behind the ball and the draw is not possible.

Fade as Against Draw

How many successful footballers can kick with only one foot? Not many. You need to be a

THE DRAW

A draw will not happen if you are aiming too much to the left in the set up, if your hips are to the left of the target, or the hands are too much in front in relation to the ball, or finally, if your weight is too much on the left.

The ball should be placed to the right, with the clubface slightly closed; the body remains behind the ball, the hips and shoulders turn better to gain distance.

THE FADE

There are certain prerequisites necessary to achieve a fade (left to right trajectory). One of these is easy to put into practice: the three fingers of the left hand should grip the club shaft more tightly to avoid the face being too closed.

THE HOOK

Suppose you want to avoid a hazard, a tree, for example. This is what to do: aim at a point to the right of the obstacle and align yourself accordingly. Use a neutral grip, i.e. standard. Place the ball near the right foot. Slightly close the club face. Lift the club normally to barely inside the target line. Follow-through on impact, the face of the club having an inside-to-outside trajectory, so imparting a right-to-left spin to the ball.

rounded player as much in golf as in football. In principle, a fade gives more control of the ball. For this reason Lee Trevino, whose natural shot was a hook, preferred to change the way he played and adopted a fade, in much the same way as Ben Hogan did several years before.

The fade is recommended for those players who hook rather than draw the ball. Another advantage of the shot is that if the fade goes wrong, and a slice is produced, it's generally less serious than a bad hook. As Trevino used to say: "You can talk to a fade, but a hook won't listen to you." The fade is well suited to many modern courses with their raised greens. It is also an undeniable advantage to heavier players who experience difficulty in turning. The fade stops better on the green, as the ball lands more softly. These are the pros. The main disadvantage of the fade is that it decreases the length of the shot.

The draw. Tests have shown that the draw carries the ball further than the fade. This is understandable. The open clubface produces a lateral effect and sends the ball higher but not as far. The swing used for the draw is more solid than that for the fade. And if the difference in length lacks importance in the case of players who can drive 250 or 260 yards (230–240 m), it

has much more significance for those whose drives do not normally reach 200 yards (180 m).

Another argument put forward in favour of the draw: although you may be in the rough, for example, isn't it preferable to play a second shot with an 8 iron than with a 6 iron?

The player who wants to stop the ball quickly needs solid contact. The draw, a shot played on the inside in relation to the line of flight, may produce less of the well-known backspin effect.

It is always hard to resolve this kind of debate. Let's say that each type of shot has its advantages. Without wanting to be too non-committal, it is better to cultivate one's natural tendency and play to one's strong points, while knowing how to achieve the reverse shot if the need arises. Something on which everyone will agree is that the straight shot is the safest of all – definitely the most accurate and invariably the longest. Draw your own conclusions!

High Ball

You have to be able to play all kinds of shots in golf. For example, your ball is behind a copse of trees. You need to be able to get through, i.e. over this obstacle if you want to carry on. To do so,

adjustments will need to be made to the set up. As regards the rest, you will need to be as relaxed as possible and follow-through well after impact. When setting up, the ball is positioned a little in front, and the hands slightly behind, which will increase the openness of the clubface (already slightly open). The swing need not be modified.

Low Ball

Before deciding if you can get past an obstacle, study the lie first. If it is good, you can think about the best way to proceed. Don't forget either that if there are trees to be avoided with the second shot, there is likely to be a bunker awaiting by the green. It is therefore preferable to play short on occasions, even if it means playing another full approach shot to get to the green.

When setting up, place the ball near the right foot. Your hands are in front of the ball. The weight is more on the left and you grip the club slightly lower down the shaft. Under these conditions, you should hit a ball with a low trajectory. The swing should be more compact than usual, a little foreshortened, and the same applies to the follow-through. But don't be too fussy!

TO LOFT THE BALL LIKE
IAN WOOSNAM IN THIS
PHOTOGRAPH, IT IS BEST
TO POSITION IT SLIGHTLY
IN FRONT, WITH THE
HANDS SLIGHTLY
BEHIND. ABOVE ALL,
DON'T TENSE UP.

ERRORS

What is the difference between the very good player and the average player? Among other things, it is the knowledge of where you are going wrong. A player makes a great step forward on the day when he knows why his ball has gone in one direction rather than another. But it's true to say that even champions sometimes don't know the causes of their mistakes. That is no reason not to attempt to find out. Golf is a perpetual quest, and video analysis has greatly helped things in recent years. It now enables a golfer to put his finger on what is going wrong, even if that in itself does not solve the problem.

Knowing how to turn your mistakes to good account means making your game work for you.

The Slice

In contrast with the fade, the slice is generally uncontrolled. Its trajectory is left-to-right. It could be said to be the golfer's disease, as 75 percent of players suffer from it. There are two basic essentials which need to be understood with regard to side spin: the swing plane and the alignment of the clubface at impact. When these two factors intervene, either individually or both

UNFORTUNATELY ALL
ERRORS INVOLVE THEIR
OWN PUNISHMENT.
THERE ARE A THOUSAND
AND ONE ERRORS IN
GOLF, ALL OF WHICH
NEED THE APPROPRIATE
THERAPY.

together, the ball is sliced every time. All the causes of a slice, and they are numerous, start from this basic premise. There is also a third factor linked to the other two – a very steep angle of attack.

Causes
– clubface too open when addressing the ball;
– the grip is too weak, one hand is too far to the left of the club shaft, which necessarily opens the clubface during the swing;
– the ball is placed too far toward the left foot, creating an open body position;
– the stance is too open, leading to an outside-to-inside swing plane;
– wrists are cocked in the takeaway, thus opening the clubface;
– left wrist cocked too much at the top of the backswing, opening the clubface;
– right leg too stiff during the backswing, preventing the left knee from sliding toward the ball, and causing it to point to the left. The natural hip movement which should accompany the body transfer from right to left is spoilt. The club trajectory is outside-to-inside;
– starting the downswing with the shoulders is a serious error but is often only a result of what has preceded it.

These causes overlap and produce different effects, with one end result: the slice.

One of the most common errors is using too much wrist at the start of the backswing, with the clubhead traveling outside the line of flight right from the start.

This has the following consequences: the ball goes to the left then to the right, due to the swing plane. The open face produces a lateral left-to-right effect on the ball which accentuates its flight to the right.

And, remember, we said golf was a sequence....! The main cause of a slice starts with the backswing.

If we had to draw the profile of the average slicer-golfer, we could distinguish four categories: the player with too strong a left side and left arm in particular; the man or woman (and this often applies to women), with far too upright a swing, who does not turn and whose arms work independently of the rest of their body; the third category of players, who, due to their weight, do not get into a position which enables them to pivot properly and finally, those with a poor posture position, either too straight, or leaning too far forward. All these golfers will have a problem

SLICE

RIGHT SHOULDER TOO FAR IN FRONT
A player often thinks he is correctly aligned when, in fact, his feet, hips and shoulders are all pointing to the left of the target. Hence a pronounced slice. This is a common error and is easy to correct. It is sufficient to visualize the line before each shot, and to take care that one's feet are quite parallel with this line. The rest follows. The right shoulder should be slightly back, in a more relaxed position.

SLICE ANTIDOTE
There are no end of reasons for the slice but equally there are numerous remedies. One such remedy consists of using some string with a weight at one end. Make the same swing as if you had a club in your hand. When the weight reaches the lowest point of its arc, you will hear the familiar whistling sound which accompanies the follow-through. Practice swinging the weight slowly, just enough for the string to be straight and to achieve its maximum speed when it reaches the ground. Then take a club and do the same thing. You will soon notice that your forearms move through more easily, with the right hand above the left in the impact zone, and the strike will also be more inside-to-outside and not the opposite. You might be surprised to find that you play a controlled draw which sends your ball into the middle of the fairway.

SEPARATE YOUR HANDS ON THE CLUB
To kill a slice, try to play a hook. Take an open club and separate your hands on the shaft with the right hand low. Don't turn your shoulders; lift on the inside.

SLICE ANTIDOTE
One of the causes of the slice is too upright a movement, with a swing plane which is too outside-to-inside in relation to the target. To correct this, address the ball with the toe of the club; this will have the effect of distancing you from the ball and producing a more inside swing plane.

SWING IN AN ARMCHAIR
You will never correct your slice unless your swing plane begins on the inside and follows through

with slicing at some point.

The slice is a fairly complex matter. For example, there is not just one kind of slice, but three. First, there is the ball which leaves straight, but because it has a high trajectory, bears to the right at the end of its flight (this can be explained by leaning over the ball too much in the set up, with the head down). The most common type could be called the "pull slice," with a left trajectory at the start and a right trajectory at the finish — this is typical of the natural slicer, who tries to direct the ball more to the left so as not to play to the right, and in doing so accentuates his tendency to slice the ball. Finally the "push-slice" is similar to the hook, in that it is a slice which goes from bad to worse.

It is important to suggest effective remedies for all kinds of slice. This is what we are going to do now.

Remedies

In the set up, when the body is pointing to the left of the target, and the right hand is too high up the shaft; when the weight is too much to the left and on the heels, and the ball too far in front with the arms and the upper body too straight, or when the club has risen too quickly, instead of staying close

the ball, with the club face square at impact. Sit on a chair and hold a club parallel with the ground at the height of your navel. With the top half of the body motionless, swing as if you were in your normal position. During the backswing, the right arm bends while the left passes above it. In the downswing, the reverse happens.

RELAX YOUR RIGHT ARM
Whether you hit a pulled hook or a slice, ask yourself the same question: "Is my set up position correct?" Often too much emphasis is placed on the right

side – the right shoulder is too high and on the outside, and the right hip is aimed too much at the ball. Rotation will be hindered. Take up your normal set up position again with a slightly higher left shoulder and more relaxed right arm.

THE TEE THAT SAVES
If you tend to hit sliced shots, try this tip: put a tee in the grass about two and a half feet (80 cm) beyond the ball to the right. Hit it with an 8 iron, trying to direct the clubhead toward the tee at impact. Place the tee further away if you are using a

to the ground – when all or some of these phenomena occur at the same time, the slice happens automatically.

To put matters right, you need to find out what is wrong first of all, and work at your weakness(es). You should check the points below one by one:
– memorize the muscles which need to work in order to produce a draw or a straight shot rather than a slice;
– achieve or regain a good set up position, with the clubface directed at the target, the body aligned in parallel with it, a neutral grip with the hands linked, weight slightly forward and to the right, the top of the body leaning so that the arms can swing freely, and the right side lower and relaxed.

Then check this list:
– a neutral grip; stance which is not too wide; ball position in the centre of the feet;
– not too far away from the ball;
– clubface directed toward the ball to waist height; no sway;
– the clubface at the top of the backswing should be half closed, and the right wrist should be under the club shaft;
– backswing with clubhead inside the line of

longer club. You will get into the habit of modifying the swing plane, which will become inside-to-outside. It has to … and you will become a drawer of the ball.

STATE OF THE TEE: A SIGN
When using the driver, you should never break your tee, nor even hit it into the air. If you do, it's because your angle of approach is too vertical. Try the following tip to correct it: put a ball on a tee and place the driver behind it, then voluntarily shadow three or four swings which pass over the ball without touching it. Put the club in position again and now try

to play the ball without touching the tee. This should give a good idea of a successful approach angle with a driver contacting the ball as it rises again, and not in the descending arc.

ALIGNMENT

ALIGN YOURSELF BETTER
Often a well hit ball does not go straight. Frequently this is to some degree due to poor alignment. A simple piece of advice can help you to regain confidence quickly. After addressing the ball, stand up, and take the club to waist height with the end of the club pointing

flight, on the inside as it comes down, on the outside at impact and follow-through.

The hook

The golf swing is full of contradictions. Just think that in order to send the ball into the air, you need to hit it as you come downward. To send it to the right, you have to come from the outside to the inside. To send it to the left, which is what we will deal with now, you have to go from the inside to the outside. In addition, if you ask a player who normally hits a slice to play a hook, the change isn't so obvious, in so far as he is in fact being asked to hit the ball to the right. Yet that's the only way to play a hook.

Causes
Like the slice, the hook is a serious error, even if its reputation does not seem to be as bad as that of the former. There are three reasons for it: a closed clubface at impact; the top half of the body remaining too much behind the ball when it is hit and an inside-to-outside plane in relation to the line of flight in the downswing.

The closed face at impact is explained by the hand action being too strong; before impact, the player's hands will turn anticlockwise excessively. The hands cannot move freely unless you stay well behind the ball.

The third condition is equally vital. If the plane were outside-to-outside, this would produce a pulled hook, i.e. a shot which would start off going to the left, and subsequently move even farther in that direction. The same result is produced if the swing plane is outside-to-inside in relation to the line of flight with the clubface open at impact.

This kind of hook has little in common with the true hook, which has a trajectory where the ball starts off going to the right or slightly to the right, and then curves in to the left.

Remedies
To understand the role of the closed clubface, take a club and place it behind a ball, turning the wrists to the left. You will see that the toe of the club is ahead of the heel and that the openness has been reduced. You have modified the angle of the clubface. Why is the clubface closed at impact? Because it is already closed at the top of the backswing, for two reasons: incorrect grip or bad backswing. Check your grip first. You should only be able to see two or two and a half knuckles

THIS IS WHAT OFTEN HAPPENS WHEN A PLAYER TRIES TO HIT A DRIVE TOO HARD. THE HOLE IS NOW EXTREMELY TRICKY TO NEGOTIATE. CAUTION IS CALLED FOR. THINK ABOUT YOUR SCORE CARD!

in the direction of the target, parallel to the ground. Notice the imaginary extension line and aim at the hole. You will soon find out if your alignment is wrong.

BACKSWING

SWING IS TOO FLAT
Are you familiar with shots that start off low and veer to the right? They happen because the swing plane is too flat. So that at the top of the backswing your hands are underneath and outside the right shoulder. Result: the clubface is never square upon impact. Solution: use a more upright swing with a

hand position above the right shoulder and the club pointing more to the target.

SUPPLE LEFT ARM
Too much tension in the swing: when a player's rhythm is too quick, his swing is often too short, with insignificant rotation. In the downswing, the hands work too much to generate clubhead speed. The clubface closes with a resultant bad shot. To eliminate this, try to keep your left arm more supple, and this will control the speed of the club. The left arm should then fall naturally toward the ball

during the downswing. Later, when you have got used to this feeling, your left arm can become more active, with perhaps a more pronounced knee action. But as soon as problems reappear, go back to basics and think of your left arm, which should have the maximum suppleness.

TRAJECTORY: CLOSE THE FACE
Hold the club with the left hand only. Close the clubface, then open it again. Repeat this several times. Then, still using one hand, start the backswing, with the hand just going past the

right leg. Carry out the swing as if you had a ball. Start again with both hands, still keeping the idea of closing the club with the left hand. After a few practice sessions, you should be able to improve the trajectory of your shots.

LEFT WRIST LOCKED
A common error is to open the clubface during the backswing. The left wrist then arches at the top of the swing. To eliminate this problem, the ideal solution might be to fasten a piece of wood on to the wrist and back of your left hand.

on the left hand, and the right hand should not be round the shaft or under it. If it is too far underneath, correct it by recreating the familiar V which is formed when the thumb and index finger extend directly in line with the club shaft.

In general, it is the right hand which is the culprit. When it is under the shaft, it controls the left hand and closes the clubface. And you know that the left side is fundamental in golf.

As for the swing, if it tends to be flat, it assists in opening the clubface in the backswing with often excessive compensation during the downswing, the hands turning anticlockwise. The combination of a bad grip and a bad swing make it very hard to cure a hook. The player with a swing which is too flat should attempt to complete the backswing in one movement, thinking of the letter Y being formed by the two arms and the club. It is vital for the club to remain close to the ground at the start.

Another thing to keep an eye on is your stance. To correct a hook, the stance should open slightly and allow the shoulders to become perpendicular to the line of flight.

The ball position does not change. It should be slightly toward the right foot for an approach shot, and nearer the left foot for the longer club.

To sum up, the hook is definitely an error, but it is essentially an exaggerated form of what should really take place. Think about it.

If you hook the ball, check: your grip (it should be neutral); your clubface (it shouldn't be closed at the top of the backswing); your backswing (it shouldn't be too flat); your stance (which should be slightly open).

You should also be aware that in certain situations there is some advantage in hitting a hook, just as there can be in hitting a slice. There is no need to expand greatly on this. Suffice it to say that you should pivot well, that it is the lower part of the body which works, that you should hit the ball through the line of flight, keep your head behind the ball and roll your wrists quickly on impact.

The push

Of all the types of spin which can be imparted to the ball, the push is the least discussed. It occurs less frequently than its opposite number, the pull.

In fact, the push is almost a good shot, since it exaggerates what should be done, rather like the hook. The trajectory of the ball is straight. It starts on the right and finishes on the right, keeping the

DON'T TOUCH THE GROUND WITH THE CLUB
If your wrists cock too soon during the backswing, try to keep the club slightly above the ground when addressing the ball. This will force you to stay close to the ground at the start of the backswing.

LIFT THE LEFT SHOULDER
If you feel that your left shoulder drops too much during the backswing, take a driver and play with it horizontally at shoulder height. When you have absorbed this new movement, get lower little by little until you

swing normally. The left shoulder drops slightly and forms a plane with the arm perpendicular to the spine.

THE "FLYING ELBOW"
More and more golfers have a right elbow which moves away from the body during the backswing. This is undoubtedly the result of an attempt to gain more distance. To avoid this movement, you need to feel that you are starting the backswing with the left arm touching the chest and the hands touching the right shoulder. The rotation will then be complete. The swing

plane will be flatter.

PLAY BASEBALL
Sway is lateral movement during the backswing. It causes loss of accuracy and, above all, loss of clubhead speed and therefore loss of power. To feel your hips turning with your shoulders, address the ball with the club about twelve inches (30 cm) above the ball and rotate like a baseball player, even if you feel the backswing is flat (this is only an impression).

Then lay the club on the ground and try to regain the same feeling by lifting the club.

DOWNSWING

FALLING ON THE BALL
To avoid falling on the ball at impact, you need a good backswing. There are various ways of achieving this. One way consists of lifting the right heel before commencing the backswing and putting it back down when making the downswing.

TO AVOID TOPPING THE BALL
One of the most common errors is to hit the top of the ball in the downswing. All coaches condemn this, and you yourself probably haven't escaped the scourge. If so, imagine that a

same direction throughout its flight.

The push is produced when the swing plane of the clubhead is too inside during the backswing and too outside after impact, with the clubface quite square in relation to this line. This means that if the plane is outside during the downswing and at impact, the clubface is automatically open. It is true that it resembles the hook in so far as the clubface is closed, as it is in the hook.

Why is it said to be a "good" fault? Because it is the opposite of the slice and pull, the serious problems of the golfer. Moreover, when a slicer starts to mend his ways, he often plays a push, exaggerating in the opposite direction. As with the other faults, it is important to know the cause, and then find some practical solutions.

Causes

The push is usually the result of the combined action of hands and body which are in front of the ball at impact. Equally, a flat backswing and poor ball position at address can influence its trajectory. Lastly, (sometimes it is the least obvious thing which is the cause) check that your aim is good. If you are aligned too far to the right and you are aiming to the right, then it is natural for the ball to go in this direction. It's easy but

THE MARVELOUS THIRD HOLE ON THE MAUNA KEA COURSE IN HAWAII. A PUSHED OR PULLED SHOT HERE IS LIKELY AS NOT TO END UP IN THE PACIFIC OCEAN.

heavy weight is attached to the top of the grip at the start of the downswing. You have to tow it downward with the club, so it is vital to pull the club and not put the head of the club first. The point is that the angle formed by the left arm and the club remains constant for as long as possible so that the ball is whipped up to maximum effect at impact.

ARMS EXTENDED
Instead of having an outside-to-inside swing plane, which tends to create a slice, it is important to start the backswing in a plane which is closer to the extension of the ball and to do the same during the downswing. This implies that the arms form an extension both for the backswing and the downswing.

PROBLEMS WITH TRAJECTORY: ANALYZE YOUR DIVOT
A badly directed shot can be explained by two phenomena: either the club face is open or closed at impact, or the swing plane is bad.

If your divot is clearly to the left, it means that your swing plane is outside-to-inside in relation to the ball, probably because the top of the body acts first during the downswing and pulls the arms to the left.

If the divot points to the right, the plane must be inside-to-outside, and the body hasn't turned enough to the left during the downswing. The solution in both cases: play with your feet together for a short time. If your divot goes straight but the result is still the same, i.e. a badly directed shot, it's due to the position of the clubface at the point of impact: if the ball ends up going left, the clubface was closed, and vice versa. In this case, check your grip. The back of your left hand and the palm of your right hand should be directed toward the target. If your grip is not the cause, perhaps another tip can help you. If your clubface is too closed, play a few balls releasing your right hand from the club after impact. The right side will not predominate and the clubface will not be too closed. If the clubface is open, do the opposite. Try to play a few balls with the right hand only on the club. You will feel a sensation of the face being open to start with, then square and then closed after impact.

PRECEDING PAGES:
A GOLF COURSE
CREATED IN THE
MIDDLE OF THE
DESERT: THE FAMOUS
LA QUINTA RESORT,
NEAR PALM SPRINGS,
CALIFORNIA.

useful to check.

The reason for adopting a position which is too far in front of the ball can be explained by one of two faults: either the swing has commenced with the ball positioned too close to the right foot, or lateral movement to the left has occured during the downswing. In either circumstance, the clubface cannot be square. Sway during the downswing is often caused by sway during the backswing. It acts as a kind of compensation. Bad ball position is easily put right. If the backswing is too flat, the clubface has every chance of being open at the top of the backswing. To avoid this, keep close to the ground at the start of the backswing to make it slightly more upright and to achieve a squarer clubface.

Remedies

Check that you are not swaying. Let the clubhead drop and remain behind the ball. Check your grip and stance, and check that your backswing is not flat. Check the ball position during address too.

The pull

There is nothing more frustrating than thinking you have hit a good shot, only to see it sailing off to the left. It is more serious when you send the ball in completely the opposite direction to the one intended. We are not talking about the compromises you make when the ball is hit straight.

The pull occurs when the ball starts off to the left of the target line and continues in that direction.

Causes

They are very similar to the causes of the slice, as these two faults are close cousins. There is a variation on the pull which is called the "pull-hook," characterized by a ball trajectory to the left, which is accentuated at the end of its flight. You've got it – the pull is the exact opposite of the push. Push and hook, pull and slice, it's the same old struggle. The difference between the push and the slice is explained by a square clubface at impact in the first case, and an open one in the second. Both the pull and the slice have an outside swing plane during the backswing. If you close the clubface, you will produce a pull-hook.

Remedies

After reviewing the main principles of the grip, set up, stance and alignment, as a matter of

TOP

CURE IT WITH A TEE
If you are prone to topping the ball, try the following practice exercise to eliminate it: place a tee about twelve inches (30 cm) from the ball. Pretend that the real tee is the one placed in front. You will learn to keep the club close to the ground for longer.

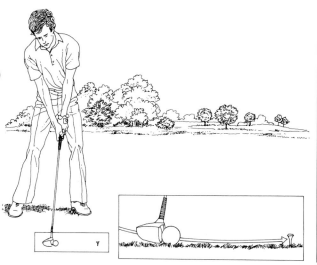

STRETCH THE LEFT ARM
One reason for topping the ball is lifting the club too quickly, hence lack of width in the swing arc or rotation of the shoulders. All you can do at the top of the backswing is to compensate with your hands in the downswing. To put this right, think about keeping the club and left arm close to the ground at the start of the backswing. The shoulders will turn better and you will have a better sweep in the downswing instead of using the upper body only.

course, check that you are not positioned too far away from the ball. If this is the case, your movement is liable to be too flat, with an outside-to-inside trajectory and a ball hit with the toe of the club.

Next, check that the top of your backswing is correct. Think of making an all-in-one movement, as described in the previous chapters. Think also of pivoting your shoulders and hips correctly.

How do you carry out the downswing?
Above all, don't force the club and try to come down on the inside. Swing the clubhead and transfer body weight correctly. Follow-through well. Lots of basic points already covered, but which need to be constantly reviewed.

The top

It is a commonly held belief that only bad players top the ball. Although it's true that most of them do, occasionally good players hit some resounding tops too! You will also notice that the ball is generally topped in places where it shouldn't happen, such as when there are water hazards, or trees to avoid, or some other unpleasant hindrance. The obstacle is therefore more psychological than anything else.

When one seeks to explain the reasons for a top, one finds at least three triggering factors: moving the head; straightening up; sway. The result is that the angle of attack is bad. These three factors may be involved all at the same time or independently.

The head
This is the most frequent cause of topping the ball. It is so tempting to look to see where the ball has gone that you raise your head before impact. Yet raising the head is only the result of the premature action of the upper body when it modifies the pivot axis. The shoulders are the origin of head movement. Slow down the backswing and be more relaxed.

Sway
A player often moves during the backswing by trying to pivot properly. The swing arc therefore moves several inches. Result: the club makes contact with the ball as it is coming up again, which means that it only touches the top.

Body straightens too early
This is often a result of compensation. The player

SWAY

ANTIDOTE TO SWAY: PUT SOMETHING UNDER YOUR FEET
Sway (lateral body movement) is insidious. The player is not immediately aware of it, yet it has very perverse results. There is a good way of preventing sway during the backswing. Practice your backswing with a ball under the outer side of your right foot. This locks the body and you cannot sway. Keep the ball there as long as you feel susceptible to this error.

DON'T SLIDE TO THE RIGHT
There are various ways of overcoming sway. One way is simply to ask a friend to hold a club at hip height on the right side in order to check whether your hip slides to the right during the backswing.

Obviously the club will move if you are swaying.

Another method of avoiding sway is to imagine that there is a cliff edge just by your right side, and that it is vital not to slide toward it.

A STICK ON THE OUTSIDE
If your right leg is not in the same position at the top of the backswing as it was when addressing the ball, you need to correct it. One good method is to put a stick into the ground on the outside of your right foot. If your left knee touches it during the backswing it's because you are moving. Practice!

You can also rest an iron against your right leg. If the club falls during the backswing, it's because you've still got a lot of work to do.

BALANCE

FEET TOGETHER
If you feel that the top of your body moves during the backswing, practice with your feet together. Your shoulders and arms will turn first. Don't widen your stance until you get the correct feel.

may have leant too far forward when addressing the ball. The transfer was incorrect and the club lifted badly.

Remedies

As regards the head, we have already seen that it is necessary to slow down the rhythm of the backswing as much as possible. As for sway, make sure that the club rises on the inside. Your body will then pivot more easily.

As regards straightening up, take care not to lean over too far when addressing the ball, and not to be too far away from it.

There is one more reason for topping the ball: when you try to snatch at the ball, for example if you have to get over a bunker. Cocking the left wrist is not the answer. Have confidence in your club and its openness. Nothing is achieved by "helping it."

Shanking or socketing

It is impossible to write a book on golf technique without discussing the shank, an affliction which is so hard to get rid of once you are suffering from it. It attacks all golfers at some time or other, and it is advisable to know how to protect against it or to get rid of it if it catches you by surprise. Having seen a professional player in a tournament run up a score of 20 on a hole after suffering from an attack of shanking I can tell you that you should never mock a golfer who is prey to it! Let's get right to the point and try to find out the real cause of the problem.

Causes

First of all, shanking (or socketing) happens when the ball is hit with the heel of the club instead of the center of the face. There are two reasons for this: the most common is exaggeration of the inside-to-outside swing plane, combined with stiff wrists which put the heel of the clubface forward. The great problem with shanking is that its effect is cumulative. This is why doubt enters the golfer's mind so quickly, and soon he doesn't know which way to turn. Even Saint Andrew abandons him.

Shanking often happens when a player has to deal with a tricky situation. He tenses up, tightens his swing and does everything back to front. The other reason is that the clubface is left open at impact due to a too flat backswing. If this is your style of shanking, there is a simple cure: get closer to the ball, and your swing immediately

---

SHANKING

HELP!
Enlist the help of a friend in your fight against shanking. Give the friend a club and ask him or her to lay it against the back of your left hand when addressing the ball. Then carry out the swing, without moving your friend's club at all. During the downswing, you should concentrate so that your left hand hits your friend's club at the same time as your club makes contact with the ball.

◄ SWING ON ONE FOOT
One of the main causes of shanking is an excessive tendency to start the downswing with the top of the body, leaning the right shoulder toward the ball. To avoid this, learn to swing on one foot, the left one, while lifting the right. You will be obliged to follow through better and your right shoulder will no longer drop. This is a good exercise for balance. If you find it difficult to carry out the whole swing standing on one leg, lift the right foot at impact only.

TWO BALLS FOR SETTING UP
Shanking can be caused by a swing plane which is too flat, or a follow through too far from the target line. When setting up, put two balls side by side. You should hit the closer one. When addressing the ball, the club is behind the second ball. The aim is to hit the first ball without touching the second. This should help you to make better contact with the ball.

becomes more upright. Insure that the ball is in a good position, preferably to the left.

Shanking can also hit you if you are off balance or because your head moves.

Remedies
– If you have a bad swing plane, try to make it more upright.
– If you use your shoulders and hands too much, release the right hand after impact.
– If you are too tense, use a lighter grip.
– If your swing plane is too inside-to-outside, try to make it more outside-to-inside.
– And of course, check all the basic principles.

The thinned shot

Causes
This type of shot is once again familiar to us all. Have we ever tried to analyze it? Probably not. Yet there is an explanation for the thinned shot. It is because the clubface is closed at impact, because the grip is wrong, the position at the top of the backswing is incorrect, the body moves sideways to the left, the hands are in front of the ball. All these reasons can produce a ball which never rises. The annoying thing is that the more

---

GRIP

WORN GLOVE: A SIGN
What state is your glove in? If the upper right part shows signs of wear, it's probably because you are holding the club wrongly in your left hand. Perhaps you are not holding it tightly enough with your fingers. At the top of the backswing, the fingers do not grip the club tightly enough and the glove is rubbed. To correct this, using the same worn glove, try to hold the club so that the worn part is visible. It will make you hold the club tighter with your fingers.

WORN GRIP: A SIGN
What state is the grip on your club in? Perhaps you have noticed that it is worn in some places. If it is, ask yourself why. It is bound to be because your movement is too quick. At the top of the backswing you lose control of the club – you are only holding it with the thumb and index finger – and during the downswing you unconsciously grip it again. It is this friction which wears your grip. To eliminate this, take three balls and hit them one after the other, each with a different rhythm; the

lift you try to give the little white devil, the more it insists on staying level with the daisies. What can be done?

Remedies

Having analyzed the causes of this problem, we must work out the consequences. In other words:
– modify your grip if necessary: check the position of your hands and revert to the familiar V (see the chapter on "Grip"). If the position at the top of the backswing is bad, check that the wrist of the right hand is well under the shaft at this point;
– if you sway, try to keep your head behind the ball during the swing;
– if the backswing is too vertical, the downswing will be on the outside of the line of flight and it is important for the backswing to be more on the inside;
– if your ball is too far to the right in the set up, the clubface risks being closed at impact. Place it closer to the center.

Skying the ball

There is no need for a diagram to show what this means! The difficulty, as with nearly all other

THE WILSHIRE COURSE IN LOS ANGELES, CALIFORNIA. NOTE THE MANICURED GREEN AND THE CREEK – TYPICAL INGREDIENTS OF MODERN GOLF.

first, at a third of the normal speed, the second at two-thirds speed, the third at normal speed. Only in this way will you learn the ideal grip and speed. It is fair to say that most of us would benefit from playing at a third of our normal rhythm.

LEFT HAND TOO FAR LEFT ▶
If your grip is incorrect, it is hard to play good shots. One of the main faults is a grip which is too weak, with the left hand too much on the left of the shaft. The V formed by the left thumb and index finger points toward

the left shoulder too much. By turning the left hand to the right on the shaft, the clubface will be better aligned with the target and the slice effect should disappear.

RELAX YOUR GRIP
If you feel that your grip is tensing up for some reason, pause for an instant and squeeze a golf ball between your thumb and the index finger of your right hand.

You will soon feel more relaxed.

FOR A LESS ACTIVE RIGHT HAND
If your right hand is too active, with the result that it goes too far up the shaft, i.e. toward the clubhead during the downswing, use a normal grip for the left hand and use only the thumb and index finger of the right hand. Start by taking a few short practice swings and learn to keep the left side dominant.

If you notice the same thing on your approach shots, practice playing with the left hand, with the right hand supporting it.

errors, lies in the confusion arising from all the different factors that are liable to give rise to skying. When trying to apply all these hypotheses to each individual case, it is sometimes hard to make sense of them.

At least the reasons for skying the ball are known:
– hitting the ball too hard; the backswing is too upright, and pivot virtually non-existent;
– swaying during the backswing, with the body weight on the left, and a falling left shoulder;
– having the weight too much on the right side at impact;
– snatching at the ball to lift it more easily;
– swinging the club from the start of the downswing;
– opening the clubface during the backswing.

In contrast with the topped shot, the club touches the bottom part of the ball. To prevent this, it is vital to iron out any errors that may have crept into the swing. Make your weaknesses disappear – the previous lessons should help you.

Fluffing

While we are on the subject of disasters, let's continue in the hope that things will become a bit

74

clearer. No examination of golfing errors can exclude fluffing. Even if this is the result of errors we have previously delved into in preceding chapters, it is important to reassure people who suffer from fluffing that it is not serious, and can easily be put right.

Fluffing is when the club touches the grass before it makes contact with the ball. You don't have to be a genius to work out that the angle of attack is wrong. The swing arc has already reached its lowest point and rises again when the ball is struck. Unfortunately, if you hit the grass first, you lose a great deal of power.

Causes?

The movement is incorrect at the start, and the backswing is bound to be the reason – too quick, wrists cocked too soon, poor transfer of weight and sway to the right.

In short, the same causes, which don't always produce the same effects. There may also be a problem with the grip or stance. It needs to be studied carefully.

One should also differentiate between long and short shots. The causes of fluffing are not always the same. In short shots, the player often forgets to lift the ball into the air, or is afraid of being unable to do so. He snatches at it as a result, probably cocking the left wrist and his legs collapse instead of staying stable and balanced. All this has to be put right.

Remedies
– Don't forget to stay close to the ground at the start of the backswing.
– If you tend to move to the left during the backswing, try to keep your head over the ball.
– Think of transferring your weight to the right side during the backswing, and to the left for the downswing.
– Don't drop your shoulders, especially the left one, during the backswing.
– To avoid snatching at the ball, place your hands slightly in front of the club when addressing the ball.

ONLY PRACTICE WILL
ELIMINATE YOUR
ERRORS AND IMPROVE
YOUR GAME – PROVIDED
THAT YOU WORK
REGULARLY AND
CORRECTLY.

THE SWING
10 questions

Should you Cock the Wrists during the Backswing?

The action of the wrists and forearms during the backswing is important in so far as it influences the rest of the movement. Difficulty arises because there are two schools of thought on this subject. Although the majority of good players wait till the last moment to cock their wrists during the backswing, there are a number of golfers who play successfully by doing so very early.

If you wait for too long, your arms and body will still be rotating and will prejudice the downswing, as the wrists will have only just been cocked. This will lead to shoulder movement due to uncoiling too soon, and the clubhead will assume an incorrect line.

On the other hand, if you cock your wrists too soon, you may not rotate your body completely. The downswing will be made with the hands and arms only instead of with the hips and legs.

The ideal is for the shaft of the club and the left forearm to be at right-angles when the hands are at shoulder height. The downswing can only be executed correctly under these conditions, with each part of the body playing its normal role.

Cocking the wrists should not really cause any difficulty. You should do it automatically. One useful tip is to lighten your grip in the set up.

FULLY EXTENDED:
SWEDISH GOLFER, OVE
SELLBERG.

Is there a Swing for Every Individual?

In other words, can everyone hope to build their own perfect swing if they work at it?

First of all, there are certain rules or parameters which are common to all players, whether they be short, of medium height or tall. They are: a good swing plane; correct movement of the body during the downswing; good lift. These three conditions are the basis of a good swing. Nonetheless, each player should take into account his own physique, and try to make it work to his advantage.

Therefore, the shorter player will have a flatter swing, with a smaller swing arc. To compensate for this, he or she is obliged to generate speed with the hands or forearms. Take the example of the Welsh player, Ian Woosnam, who is short in stature yet propels the ball enormous distances. The player of medium height should not give preference to any one action in relation to another. On the other hand, the tall player, with a more upright swing, should not worry about his hands, but should lift the club slowly, widen his swing arc as much as possible and keep on course, i.e. maintain a good swing plane.

Women players present a special case because they invariably have less physical power than men. They need to work on their pivot and hand action to generate clubhead speed.

It is also important to check your grip each time you swing the club. If you are tall you should use a neutral grip, and if you are short you will probably need to use a stronger grip.

Head Completely Still: Illusion or Reality?

Although the basic principle of keeping your head still is written in stone, if it is taken literally, it can give rise to more difficulties than you would think.

It is important to know that each time you move your head during the swing, the swing trajectory is modified. On the other hand, if you lock your head from the address position to the finish, you will constrict your movement, which will lack width, producing a potential lack of length in the shot.

In short, you need to be supple. To clarify this, let's say that your head position should not move until the moment of impact, which doesn't mean to say keeping the chin locked. It can do no harm to imitate Jack Nicklaus, who turns his head slightly to the right immediately before he begins his takeaway. You shouldn't look up until the follow-through. This should come almost

---

FEET TOGETHER ▶

Here is a simple, but very effective test. It enables you to improve your balance and swing better on the inside of your body, so to speak. When you are practicing, play for a few minutes with your feet together. It will improve your tempo, too.

RAISE YOUR HEAD

If you move your head, try this tip. Stand where there is plenty of sunlight. Look at your shadow in front of you on the ground when you are in the set up position. With your club in place, notice where the top of your head comes on the shadow. Then check the distance between the line of the club and the actual position of the top of your head on the shadow when you play. If there is a big gap, you are still moving your head. The aim is to keep the top of your head on the shadow while you are playing, at about club height.

TWO CLUBS ON THE GROUND

To improve your leg action, and enable you to have a more effective body action, put two clubs on the ground, one slightly in front of and outside your left knee, and the other to the right and slightly in front of your head. Shadow the swing without touching either of the clubs. Your swing will be more compact and your left leg will be more solid during the follow-through and should not flex. Your whole body should move less.

naturally. A good way to practice this is to hit a few balls softly. You will find it less difficult to keep your head still. Practice making short swings, then gradually lengthening them. That head will keep still more easily!

How do you Pinch the Ball?

Before explaining how to pinch the ball to give it backspin, a word of warning – this relatively sophisticated technique is not advisable for beginners. You need to have a certain knowledge of the game and sufficient experience to be able to effect this type of shot. Professional players often use it with good results, but then they play golf every day, and (unlike most of us) rarely top or fluff the ball. You also need good playing conditions, i.e. the right kind of fairway and receptive, welcoming greens.

Without going into detail, backspin is obtained with a vertical angle of attack. The wrists cock very early and you make contact with the ball directly, even before the club touches the ground.

Five Woods and Seven Woods

The invention of lofted woods, particularly the 5 wood and the 7 wood has undoubtedly been a great help to the average golfer. But their use isn't

A REAL GOLF SHOT

If you feel your confidence draining away when you are confronted with a difficult shot to a green that is well protected by bunkers, take a few seconds to prepare yourself. Then, looking just beyond your ball, select a blade of grass as a marker and address the ball with the club using the left hand only. During the backswing, cock your left wrist and take the middle of the shaft with your right hand; lift the club normally. Now aim your left knee at the target, and come down pulling the left hand downward normally, while holding the club back with the right hand until the left hand goes past the marker. Hold that same position for ten seconds, concentrating on the spot in front of the blade of grass. Then release the right hand, follow-through normally with your left hand on the club. The finish should be about waist height. You will probably take a sizeable divot when you follow-through.

reserved exclusively for these players. Lee Trevino, for instance, will not hesitate to pull a 7 wood out of his bag when he feels the need to.

Let's take the 7 wood as an example, then, as it is now the most popular lofted wood. It allows you to get out of the trickiest situations, particularly from the rough. With a 7 wood, you can lift the ball very quickly. Open the club face and play the ball as an extension of the left heel. Its compact head allows it to penetrate the grass better than a normal iron.

Other uses: from a bad lie, on bare ground, with no turf. If you use an iron, it is virtually impossible to make contact with the ball. With a wood, you place the ball further toward the right foot and try to keep a good rhythm. Weight is evenly distributed in the set up position. But that's not all. When the ball has sunk into a divot, this shot, considered to be one of the most difficult of all, is where the 7 wood comes into its own. The ball should be in the middle of your stance, with your hands slightly in front. Don't try to pick the ball up, as the openness of the club will be sufficient to lift it. On the other hand, its trajectory is likely to be low, and it may roll further than usual. Take this into account before you play the shot.

The 7 wood is also ideal for fairway bunkers. It takes less sand than an iron. If the shot isn't completely successful, it is not a disaster. With a wood, the clubhead will tend to rebound on the sand. But don't get carried away! The ball should be lying well. If it is not, it is better to use a short iron and get back on the fairway. Check that your stance is correct. If it is not, you run the risk of losing your balance, as the swing arc of a 7 wood is wider than that of an iron. Another precaution: make sure that the lip of the bunker is not too high, as the trajectory of the shot will be quite low.

In order to play this kind of shot well, position the ball in the middle of your stance in the set up position, aim slightly to the left of the target, and use a more upright and slightly shortened swing.

Lastly, the 7 wood is often handy on a long downhill par 3, where there is a tail wind. Follow the same procedure as before, with the clubface slightly open.

The 7 wood has a wide range of uses. It would be a pity not to take advantage of them.

Should You Ground the Club at Address?
The most famous example of a player who keeps his driver off the ground in the set up is Jack

THE TOWEL
In order to hit a good swing, it is vital that the two ends of the club act in harmony. To help with this, take a towel and attach a weight to the end, a knife for example. Carry out your normal swing with it and you will notice that the knife generates power in the same way as a golf clubhead.

IF YOUR BACKSWING IS TOO SHORT

1. Before even starting the swing, adopt the following position: shoulders turned at 45 degrees, hips at 25 degrees, left knee pointing behind the ball, left heel lifted to the inside. Swing with your hands, arms and body all working together. This preparation is intended to prevent the poor position which some players adopt at the start.
2. If you don't manage to cock your wrists enough because your grip is too tight, practice hitting some balls with a short iron, without trying to hit them hard. Lift the club until the left arm is parallel with the ground and with the target line, then cock your hands so that the tip of the club is above the right shoulder and aimed at the target. In the downswing, keep your hands firm and swing your arms, trying to do the same in the downswing as you did in the backswing.
3. If your arms and shoulders are tight, put a tee into the grip end of the club shaft. Once again hit some balls with a middle iron and a light grip. Lift the club until the tee is pointing directly behind you. Conversely, after impact, the tee should be pointing in front of you in the direction of the target. Repeat this several times with your arms and hands without using your body too much.

ONE-AND-TWO

A lot of players fail to make progress because of their poor timing. One secret is to say "one-and-two," which does not necessarily mean that "one" is the backswing, "and," the pause at the top and "two" the downswing. The "and" is in fact the end of the backswing and the start of the downswing. Think about it.

Nicklaus, but Nick Faldo and Greg Norman also "hover" the clubhead. Should we imitate them? The question has no definite answer, and perhaps never will.

Clearly most golfers prefer to ground their club in the set up, but one cannot ignore the arguments of those who think it preferable to keep the clubhead off the ground. They believe that it reduces tension in the hands and forearms, and that the grip is lighter. Also, the takeaway is carried out under the optimum conditions, without being hindered by the turf, and, importantly, it is easier to have an all-in-one movement, not one just using the hands.

Are you persuaded? Use your own experience and draw your own conclusions.

Do You Need to Make a Practice Swing?

The answer is "Yes," provided the practice swing is useful and effective. Unfortunately a lot of golfers simply repeat their usual mistakes in the practice swing. A common error is to consider the practice swing as a way of relaxing. There is nothing wrong in this provided the practice swing is not unorthodox, with your head following the path of the clubhead, for example.

The main virtue of the practice swing is that it

THE SHORT GAME IS OF GREAT IMPORTANCE. IT CAN TURN "THREE SHOTS INTO TWO" AND COMPENSATE FOR A DEFICIENT LONG GAME. THE SPANIARD MANUEL PINERO IS ONE OF ITS MOST BRILLIANT EXPONENTS.

LIFT YOUR LEFT LEG

Here are two exercises to enable you to appreciate the action of the legs. First: stand in the set up position without a club and turn your hips as far as you can. Second: with the same stance, lift your left leg and swing it in front of your right leg then bring it back to its initial position. People generally prefer the second exercise. Practice until this becomes second nature, then change over legs. When that in turn has become quite natural, take a club and practice hitting some balls while carrying out the exercise.

IF YOUR BACKSWING IS TOO EXTREME

You can tell if your backswing is too extreme if your left wrist is too cocked. To insure that the relationship between the clubface, the back of the left hand and the forearm stay the same at the top of the backswing, stand normally in the address position, lift the club with your hands, then lift your arms to the height of your torso. Turn your shoulders and lift your arms normally. It would be surprising if your left wrist were still cocked.

If your weight distribution is

bad during the backswing, try consciously to lift your left heel and bring it squarely in front of your right foot. Then return it to its original position while making the downswing.

If your shoulders turn badly, kneel on a stool and hit some balls with a wood. You will see that you need to turn sideways rather than up and down.

BACK TO THE TARGET ▶

There are several ways of developing the arm action during the swing. One way is to play with your feet together (see above) and risk falling over if you move your shoulders too much. Another way is to play with your back to the target. Stand normally in the set up position, then turn round so that your back is facing the target, although your left shoulder hasn't changed position. Then swing as if you were in the normal set up position. At first this may not seem obvious, but you might find it very useful.

simulates the stroke you are about to play. Therefore if the practice swing is to be effective, you need to take into account all the factors affecting the shot itself.

Once this has been memorized, choose a blade of grass and then swing the shaft of the club at it, without worrying overmuch about its speed.

The shadowed swing is meant to help practice. It is particularly advisable for certain kinds of shot: when the lie is uphill, downhill or lateral, it is a good idea to get used to the different feel. Also, if the previous shot has been a bad one, it is vital to drive away negative thoughts. Round the green, where each shot is different, it is important to visualize the type of shot you want to play. When you are waiting at the start of a hole, say a par 3, why not stand a couple of yards behind the ball and do a few practice swings as if you were really playing? Because every shot is different, it is essential to recall the right feel before playing.

A bad practice swing is worse than no practice swing at all. If this happens, don't hesitate to try again.

Wedge or Chipper around the Green?
One of the best known golfing maxims is "The important thing is not how, but how many." In other words, effectiveness comes first.

When the ball is close to the green, you often have to make a choice between two types of shot: the first means pulling out your wedge or sand wedge from your bag and hitting a shot with a high trajectory and minimum roll once on the ground; the second consists of using a fairly less lofted iron, a 7, 8 or 9 iron in most cases, and giving the ball a low trajectory with a lot of roll.

Both methods have their supporters but it is undeniable that the second is the safer shot and gives better results as a rule, although it is less spectacular. It is much more thrilling to see the ball rise and die just a few inches from the flag. The disadvantage is that this is not achieved all that often, and it requires more skill to be successful with this type of shot than with the so-called Scottish run-up. When it is windy, the first solution is no longer viable. On a links course, the second method of play always takes precedence. The swing is shorter, and the wind has less effect on the ball. If this type of shot suits you, you should use it more often. For example, if the ball is about thirty five yards (30 m) from the green with an uphill lie, it would not be unreasonable to play a 5 iron, or even a 4 iron. With practice you will soon get to like the Scottish game.

LEFT FOOT BEHIND

Stand normally in the set up position. Move your left foot just behind your right leg. Raise the club, turning your back consciously toward the target for a few moments. When you begin the downswing, raise your left foot a little and complete the swing. Your head should scarcely move.

ASK A FRIEND

To get a better feeling of lightness and suppleness in the arms, ask a friend to hold your clubhead while you hold the shaft with your left hand. Grip tightly. Ask them to swing the club.

You will both find it very hard to move it. Now, instead of gripping it tightly, adopt a light grip. Your friend will no longer have any difficulty in swinging the club. It is this light feel you need to reproduce when you play.

THREE BALLS IN A STRAIGHT LINE

The weight of the club and its acquired speed act on the arms. To appreciate this, place three balls or more on the ground in a straight line. Hit each ball one after the other without stopping. You will be surprised how easy it is. This is simply because the weight of the club and the speed it has acquired act on your arms and make it easier to hit the ball.

IN YOUR HALLWAY

Although your legs play an essential role in the downswing, they should not cause your hands and especially the club to lag behind. If this is the case, the clubface may be open at impact. The reason? Your hips have turned too soon outside the target line. In contrast, if the clubhead is in front, your leg action hasn't been strong enough. You can tell by carrying out this simple experiment: stand in the set up position in your hallway, against a door frame, take a club and place it against the wall. Then lift and swing gently. The aim is to have the club flat against the wall again at impact.

If you are practicing, try this as well: take a 7 iron out of your bag, put a ball on a tee and play a 3 to 6 yard shot (3–6 m). This should give you a (good) feel of playing with your legs.

Where Should You Position the Ball?

In the set up position you should observe the general principle that the ball should be positioned increasingly close to the left foot in proportion to the length of the club and its openness. For example, it is obvious that with a driver, the ball should be positioned as an extension of the left heel, while with a wedge, the ball should be nearer the right foot. These two extremes apart, there is a whole range of different situations needing permanent adaptation. Unfortunately, when you hit a bad shot, it is never explained away by bad ball placement.

There are four ways of positioning the ball incorrectly:

— too near the left foot: if it's a matter of a few inches, it is not serious. If it is more than this it will have negative results, probably inducing a pull or a slice. In fact, with the shoulders open, the swing plane is outside-to-inside, and the downswing is hurried;

— too near the right foot: if it's a matter of a few inches, the ball will have a lower trajectory, and that's all. If it is more than that, the shoulder alignment will be too closed, the swing plane too inside-to-outside. The result will be a push or a hook;

"GOLF," HENRY LONGHURST USED TO SAY, "TAKES US TO SUCH BEAUTIFUL PLACES"; CALIFORNIA WOULD APPEAR TO HAVE MORE THAN ITS FAIR SHARE OF BEAUTIFUL (AND EXTRAORDINARY) PLACES.

THE SWING

FOOT ACTION

Hold a club upright on the ground with your left hand. Then aim at a target and throw a ball underarm with your right hand, between the club and your body. Notice your movements with the ball, both when taking your arm back and when swinging through. You do this not just with your body but with your feet, particularly on the downswing. Try this several times. You will get a better idea of the extent to which your feet assist the balance of the swing and the accuracy of the shot. Next, take a club and imitate the swing, then hit some balls.

A TEE INSIDE YOUR LEFT HEEL

What happens if you put your left foot back down during the downswing in a different position from the one it started in? If it is further away from the right foot, it is not too serious. If it is nearer your right foot, this means that your stance has narrowed during the swing and your follow-through is liable to be outside-to-inside, which is never good. To check, put a tee just inside your left heel. If you miss the tee during the downswing, that's OK. But if you push it into the ground, you have moved your heel in the wrong direction.

CLUB ON YOUR THIGHS

Take a club and lay it against your thighs. Then make a backswing and a downswing with the club still flat against your thighs. Sometimes the shaft of the club moves away from the thighs. This simply means that the foot action is disconnected, which is not good. It's up to you to find a good rhythm.

PREDOMINANT LEFT SIDE

To avoid a predominant left side, try this tip. With the right palm perpendicular on the grip, lift the club to its highest point using only the left shoulder and forearm.

THE WATCH

Think of the face of a watch, and lift the club to 9 o'clock; check that the clubhead is pointing skyward. Swing round as far as 3 o'clock, checking the clubhead again. This will teach you to control the angle of the clubface better.

A CLOCK IN YOUR HEAD ▶

The backswing is vital for good impact. So, when addressing the ball, imagine there is a clock on the ground telling you the time. 12 o'clock represents the direction of the target.

You are at 3 o'clock. If you want to check that your swing is right, the club must pass 7 o'clock. If at the top of the backswing, the clubhead points to 6, or even worse, to 5 o'clock, it is liable to be too far left in relation to the target. You need to think about putting this right.

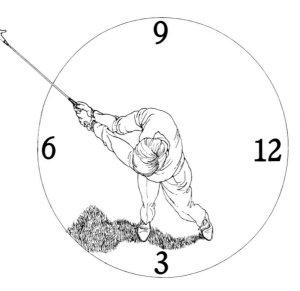

WIDEN THE SWING ARC

To widen your swing, place your right foot behind your left foot when addressing the ball, line up two clubs on the ground in front of you in the direction of the target and hit a few balls. You will notice that your hips and shoulders turn more easily. Now take up your normal stance and try to build in this new feeling. Another way of widening your swing is to use your right arm to assist you. In fact, the right arm supports the left one, or rather, the left wrist, and helps it to rise as high as possible.

– too far away: this is a common error when you try to hit the ball hard. The swing is flatter and the ball will be lower. Often the leg action is reduced and balance impaired. Result: a hook or a slice;

– too close: a less common mistake. The swing plane will be more upright, and the ball will start high. Your back will be too stiff and your knees too flexed.

A good way of checking if you are the right distance away from the ball is to stand upright with a club horizontal in front of you. Now lean forward until the club touches the ground. This is a useful exercise for any type of club. Some people think that whatever the club, the ball should always be positioned opposite the inside of the left heel. False: it demands significant leg action in the downswing and not everyone can achieve this. Also, it is much harder to keep your shoulders square at impact.

Lastly, the lie is a factor. If it is good, the ball can be played toward the left foot. If it is bad (a downhill lie, for example), the ball should be placed nearer the right foot.

Weight on the Left Foot or the Right?
It all depends on the shot you have to play.

Weight more on the right foot
The shot that requires, let's say, 90 percent of the body weight on the right side, is the short lobbed shot, where the ball rises and falls quickly.

If you want to play a hook, you should have about 70 percent of your body weight on the right when addressing the ball, but in contrast with the lobbed shot, the weight is more on the left foot at the finish.

If you are to hit a drive with the wind at your back, put 60 percent of your body weight on the right side when addressing the ball.

Weight evenly balanced on both feet
This should happen when playing out of a bunker. The weight is 90 percent on the left at the finish.

The shot into the wind with a wood
The weight is rather more on the left side in order to play a low, rolling shot.

The Scottish pitch-and-run shot is where the body weight is mainly on the left, about 90 percent when addressing the ball. This distribution of weight should not be modified when executing the swing.

A BELT AROUND YOUR ARMS ▶

Surely it's crazy to think that a belt might solve your problems! But even the great players believe it can help. You can often see them practicing with a belt wound round their arms. Why? To make their arms work together. To keep the right elbow back at the top of the backswing and to insure a good follow through, with the arms well extended. In short, when you take the belt off, everything will seem much easier.

DON'T HIT, THROW

The majority of beginners are too tense when they play and tend to use the power of their shoulders, when they should use their hands and arms more. Golf is a throwing movement. You hit the ball with your hands and not with your shoulders. To be more aware of your arms acting like a pendulum, accentuate the shoulder pivot by bracing your back muscles, take a club at each end and swing it, keeping your arms extended vertically.

Your feet should be together to keep the body well centered over the ball.

A CLUB UPSIDE DOWN

To check how well the clubhead accelerates just after impact, you can carry out a simple test. Turn a club upside down and hold it by the head. Do several swings until you can hear the whistling noise of the shaft through the air. You may hear this noise shortly after the start of the downswing, just before the estimated point of impact; in other words, just when the shaft is between shoulder and hip height. If this is the case, you have identified a problem.

It proves that you are not accelerating the clubhead at impact, or beyond. To appreciate this fully, it is necessary to repeat the exercise until you can hear the whistling of the shaft clearly when it passes hip height, just after the estimated point of impact.

POWER AND ACCURACY

Power

Golf is not a game of sheer physical strength. There is no need to be a sumo wrestler, even if Jack Nicklaus has always claimed that he hit the ball much harder when he was barely twenty and weighed about 220 pounds (100 kg).

His longtime coach, Jack Grout, made him work on power in his drive right from the start. He emphasized that "accuracy will come later, length must come first."

Like all throwing sports, it is best to have one's weight behind the ball. Generally the "heavyweights" are the longest hitters. Perhaps the best example today is the ever-popular Craig Stadter, affectionately known as "The Walrus." His great weight is not a hindrance – quite the contrary, for it enables him to hit some prodigously long shots, which is to his advantage. But to advise you to put on a little weight if you want more length on your drives is something I will not do. Because the opposite is also true. How does one explain how players like the Spaniard, Jose Maria Olazabal or the Australian, Brett Ogle can hit the ball so hard when they are as thin as beanstalks?

In golf the adversaries are the ball, the course and indirectly the person you are playing against,

EVEN IF POWER IS NOT EVERYTHING, IT GREATLY BENEFITS THE PLAYER WHO HAS IT. THIS PHOTO IS OF THE BRITISH GOLFER HOWARD CLARK, A PLAYER WHO IS CERTAINLY NOT LACKING IN THIS RESPECT.

which is often yourself.

Although I haven't got any miracle answers, there are definitely a number of tips which it is well worth remembering and putting into practice, because they are proven. Firstly, however, let's try to clarify the term "power" in golf.

There are three elements which relate to power: the speed of the clubhead, hitting the ball with the clubhead in line with the target, and a square clubhead at the moment of impact. If these three elements are not brought together at the same time, you risk losing length. What do esthetics matter as long as these three fundamental principles are fulfilled? There are some who would disown their own mothers to savor the pleasure of a 300 yard (220 m) drive!

Without resorting to that, we can certainly recommend the following tips.

– Position the ball high on the tee. This high position enables you to turn better during the backswing and to follow-through well upon impact. The ideal position would be for the ball to be above the apex of the club when it is resting on the ground. This will favor a high ball, because it will be hit either exactly at the base of the swing arc or very slightly on the rise. By contrast, if the tee is positioned low, the ball will be hit "coming down," and will not be swept through, as it is when the tee is high. Take care, however, not to set the tee too high, as you then risk skying the ball with the club going underneath.

– Keep your grip light. Sam Snead's theory of having a grip like a bird's nest, with the bird being the club, is a good one to retain. Most of your fingers should be in gentle contact with the club, except for the three last fingers of the left hand, and the middle and ring fingers of the right hand, which should grip the club firmly. This light grip allows a better follow-through with the clubhead, therefore increasing the distance.

– While we're talking about grip, we should mention that sometimes it can help for it to be strong, i.e. with the hands slightly on the right of the club. The swing will be flatter and the hand action freer.

– Keep your right foot more to the right, to make your backswing as effective as possible. During the downswing, a player can release his left side more easily and therefore follow-through better.

– Accentuate the leg movement: often, short players don't make the lower half of their body and knees work enough, in particular from the start of the downswing. Try to trigger the downswing with a turn of the left hip. As soon as

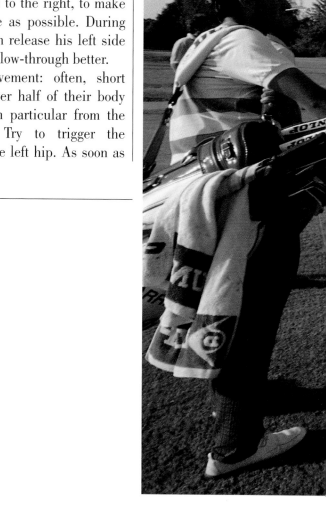

POWER CONSISTS OF
THREE ELEMENTS:
CLUBHEAD SPEED,
STRIKING THE BALL WITH
THE CLUBHEAD IN LINE
WITH THE TARGET AND
THE HEAD STAYING
SQUARE AT THE MOMENT
OF IMPACT.

your weight transfers to the left side, clear your hips. Your legs will follow.

– Let the club stay behind as long as possible and hold back your wrist action. You will then increase the width of the swing arc.

Accuracy

Golfers often prefer to be thought of as powerful players, rather than accurate ones. Yet in most cases, it is more valuable to have an accurate game. A young player should be keen to develop power, but at the end of the day, the accurate golfer has a better chance of putting in a good card. Look at the senior players, the over 50s, they are capable of producing spectacular scores, not because of their power, but because they are superb putters and accurate drivers.

What are the Prerequisites for becoming an Accurate Player?

If you adhere to the fundamental principles of the swing which have already been analyzed, you will have more chance of getting your ball on the fairway and not in the rough. Accuracy also depends on good balance, which in turn depends on good tempo.

More specifically, the swing should be more compact than when you are trying to hit the ball hard. A compact swing means a backswing where the right knee supports the body weight without slackening. This right-leg position is essential, because it controls the balance of the swing and the weight transfer.

The start of the downswing should be comparatively gentle, or the clubface may open or close and fail to be square upon impact.

Striking the ball ultimately comes down to a full follow- through. All accurate players will agree with the following:
– the grip should be neutral;
– the feet, hips and shoulders should be square or slightly open in relation to the target;
– the club should be taken away slightly on the inside and only three-quarters of the way back;
– make rhythm work;
– you should swing through the ball and not at it;
– take account of the design or layout of the hole: for example, if it is a dogleg, don't hesitate to drive up the right side of the fairway. Some players prefer not to consider potential hazards, rather they fix their gaze on a precise area of the fairway. Each to his own.

It is not enough merely to learn the secrets of becoming a good player. You must also know how to apply them.

GERMANY'S BERNHARD LANGER IS ONE OF THE MOST ACCURATE GOLFERS IN THE WORLD; HIS VERY COMPACT SWING LEAVES LITTLE TO CHANCE.

THE WISDOM OF THE CHAMPIONS

So far, we have mainly considered methods of technique directed toward the weekend golfer. This chapter is devoted to the great players of golfing history. In this context, we might ask whether we can and should be inspired by their example and by their golf swings.

Like all sports, golf has its legendary champions, such as Nicklaus, Palmer, Hogan, Jones. Each has made his own unique contribution and helped to improve the game of golf. In the 1920s, Bobby Jones was a model of tempo and rhythm. Some years later, Sam Snead underlined the importance of the arm action, while Byron Nelson emphasized the importance of the swing plane. Ben Hogan understood the role of the lower body in the downswing and Arnold Palmer embodied all that is best in the competitive player. Then there was Jack Nicklaus, who brought an almost scientific dimension to golf and Gary Player who believed physical preparation to be of fundamental importance. This brings us to the modern player, who seeks to resemble them in nearly all these qualities. Unfortunately, this typical portrait of today's champion is something akin to a robot which has no actual existence. Some come close to it, like Nick Faldo and Nick Price, but they are all ultimately human beings with their own

THE AUSTRALIAN GREG NORMAN, AN EXCEPTIONAL PLAYER WHO HAS NOT WON AS MANY MAJOR TITLES AS HIS GAME MERITS. HIS DAY MAY COME. PATIENCE IS ALSO PART OF THE WISDOM OF THE CHAMPIONS.

individual strengths and weaknesses.

If we had to draw up a list of the top ten players of all-time, no doubt it would be a very hard task, even if everyone contributed their own ideas on the subject. For example, the author's choice might include:
– Greg Norman, best driver;
– Byron Nelson, best fairway wood player;
– Jack Nicklaus, best long iron player;
– Ben Hogan, best medium iron player;
– Gene Sarazen, best approach shot player;
– Tom Watson, best chipper;
– Gary Player, best bunker player;
– Bobby Locke, best putter.

Should we copy their technique?

Certainly not. First of all, each of these champions is different. So, while their technique may be emulated, it is based on a natural talent which gives them that "special something." This makes all the difference in the world. One is born with a "special something" and it cannot be passed on. You may be surprised not to see Seve Ballesteros' name in the author's list! The reason is simple: Ballesteros is one of the most inspirational players in the history of golf. His only fault is that his game lacks consistency, which has prevented him from adding even more victories to his already impressive record of achievements. Yet, potentially, he could stand alongside Jack Nicklaus. At different times in his career, Ballesteros has been, in turn, the best driver, the best iron player, has had the best short game and been the best putter. Inspiration has flowed. But a golfer's career cannot be properly judged until it is over, so it is difficult to classify Ballesteros once and for all. He is certainly an exceptional player. Will he end up as a legend like Nicklaus, Palmer or Hogan? We'll have to wait a few more years.

When one watches a champion-in-the-making, one can believe that golf is not actually that complex. Particularly if you have never tried to hit that little white ball! Whatever one might say, it's always the same story. Two things make a really good golf shot – the position of the clubface at impact, and the trajectory of the swing. It is remarkable to find that all the champions, or nearly all, are in total agreement on this subject. More significantly, their position at impact is astonishingly similar. Yet one could never say that

GOLFING GIANTS: JACK NICKLAUS IN THE BACKGROUND AND SEVERIANO BALLESTEROS IN THE FOREGROUND. TWO PEOPLE WHO APPRECIATE HARD WORK! ENDLESS HOURS SPENT IN FRONT OF THE BALL, TRYING TO DISCOVER THE THOUSAND AND ONE SECRETS OF GOLF.

they all use identical means to achieve this, even if they adhere to the basic principles. Take the grip, for example. No champion has a bad grip. It is inconceivable. The correct position of the hands on the shaft is the basis of a good swing. From then on, from the backswing to the start of the downswing, the paths diverge, to converge again just before impact. There are examples of great players whose position at the top of the backswing has nothing to do with what is taught in the textbooks. Miller Barber, a player from the 60s, had a backswing which moved away vertically instead of laterally, allowing the body to uncoil naturally. The American Calvin Peete, one of the most accurate players on the U.S. Senior Tour, takes his club back with his left arm completely bent. Doug Sanders used to finish his backswing at hip height and the Irish player Eamonn Darcy has no fear of a flying right elbow during the backswing.

In short, everyone has their own recipe for success. Golf will always be an individual sport. The lesson to be learned lies in the fascination of watching a great player evolve, but we should not try to copy him or her. Only children have that amazing ability to imitate. On the other hand, whether you are a champion, or whether you play

only occasionally at your local club, you should make a great effort to repeat the same preparatory movements if you want to succeed. Always try to observe the same routine, which can be divided into four stages: choosing the club, visualizing the shot, setting up, and starting the swing.

The "routine"

Choice of club

This depends on several factors: whether the lie is good or bad; whether it is raining or windy; if the turf is short or long; assessment of the target – its size, and the advantages and disadvantages of playing here or there; confidence – are you sufficiently tough mentally not to be afraid of playing a difficult club?

Visualization of the shot

Stand behind the ball, facing the target. Imagine the shot you would like to play, the flight of the ball and its trajectory. Choose an intermediate target which is nearer and more easily identified.

Setting up and address

Keeping your eye fixed on the target line, stand beside the ball with your feet together. Check your grip. Move your right foot aside. Align your whole body parallel with the target line. Place the clubface against the ball. Take up your posture and stance, with the ball not too close to the left foot.

Starting the swing

Keep your intermediate target constantly in view. Use some waggle movements if you like, if you feel you need to relax. Look once more at the target, then back to the ball, and ...off you go!

THE AMERICAN CURTIS STRANGE, A TWO-TIME WINNER OF THE U.S. OPEN AND A PLAYER WHO IS RENOWNED FOR BEING MENTALLY TOUGH.

SOME SPECIAL SITUATIONS

One of the charms of golf is finding oneself (and then having to extract oneself!) from all kinds of complex situations. Each of the following examples needs special treatment.

The rough

Even if you are the most accurate player in the world, you can never pretend that you don't get into the rough. The rough reaches out invitingly to us at every hole, and it can be very difficult to avoid. How complicated we make things for ourselves! Instead of taking stock, and analyzing the situation objectively, we try to salvage a shot from the rough when, in truth, it is already lost. The rough is not the best place to catch up on lost shots. It is better to be content with a short shot, out onto the fairway, rather than ending up somewhere else in the same rough, or in a bunker or at the foot of a tree! However, there are lots of different potential situations, each with its own solution. The rough can be divided into three categories: light rough, where the ball is half sunk; thick rough, where the ball is perched; and the kind of rough where the ball is completely driven into the ground, or "plugged."

You need to appreciate the following things: that it is hazardous to try to go over a tree or a

DEEP IN THE ROUGH:
AMERICAN JOEY
SINDELAR USES HIS
EXCEPTIONAL PHYSICAL
STRENGTH TO GET
HIMSELF OUT OF THE
TRICKIEST OF
SITUATIONS.

bunker, or to want to stop the ball quickly on the green; that a shot out of the rough is hard to control, and that it is preferable in all cases to grip the club a little lower, in order to control the club more accurately.

Light rough

Don't be too bold, use nothing greater than a 5 iron, but don't hesitate to take a lower club than normal, since the low trajectory and greater roll of the ball will give it more length. The swing arc should be more upright, the wrists should be cocked sooner. In the address position, play the ball further back in the stance, which should be slightly open, and don't rest the club on the ground, so that it is not hindered by the height of the grass at the start of the backswing.

Thick rough with a perched ball

The shot looks easy. You might think it looks as if the ball is on a tee. But the danger in such a shot is to go under the ball.

What club should you use? It can range from a driver upward. Provided your technique is good. First of all, lower your grip and don't rest the club on the ground. Then play the ball closer to the right foot, in order to hit the ball on the rise. The swing arc should be as wide as possible, which is the opposite in the case of light rough. Above all, don't make a divot, but play the ball as if it were actually on a tee. Again, don't forget to use a lower club, as the ball will go further.

Thick rough with a plugged ball

This is the most extreme case, and there are few solutions to the problem. The only reasonable thing to do is to get your ball out on to the fairway, and lose a shot. To do this, you need the most open club possible, which is undoubtedly the sand wedge. The ball should be more toward the right foot. Adopt an open stance, tighter grip, upright backswing and cock the wrists quickly. Open the club face as the grass tends to close together again upon impact. And precisely at impact, the wrists must be firm – it's vital. Remember that a shot played in high grass will not have much backspin, and this should be taken into account.

Can you use a wood in the rough or semi-rough? In principle, it is not advisable to get a wood out of your bag. Most of the time, even great players hesitate to use a wood in thick rough. That shows you. On the other hand, the semi-rough can be the place to bring out your fairway

---

RECREATE SITUATIONS

It is advisable to prepare yourself well in advance for any possible situations which might arise. For example, sometimes a good drive ends up at the foot of a tree, from where it is virtually impossible to extract it using a normal swing. But don't wait until it happens on the course. While practicing, address normally; raise the club half way or three quarters of the way back; don't move, and keep your wrists cocked, with your weight on the right side. Hit the ball several times starting from this position, which means essentially using your arms and hands. Then, when this happens on the course, lift your club as far as you can, then hit normally. You have nothing to fear because you have already practiced it.

WIND: DON'T PUNCH

The punched shot is not advisable because the more you "thump" the ball, the more backspin it will have. Even if it starts low, it will soon rise quickly and lose distance. This is why players are advised to play gently, and not allow the wind to take the ball too easily.

THE DRIVER IN THE WIND

The wind forces the golfer to adapt. You need to take special care when using your driver. If you use it incorrectly, you will be prey to all kinds of potential disaster. You need to consider the following things when using your driver in the wind: your grip on the club should be about an inch lower, the backswing should be shorter, as should the follow-through, and the ball should be hit more slowly. In the set up, the ball should be slightly to the right, with a normal stance, and the hands in front of the club.

WIND: STAY IN CONTROL

To stand up to the wind, you need to counter it. You do this by hitting the ball more softly, and not hesitating to use one or two clubs more than normal, even in a side wind; in other words, by being patient, and telling yourself that the wind is just another part of the game.

Don't tense up when the wind blows. That's the worst thing you can do.

driver if you have one. Because of its flatter head, it penetrates the grass more easily, and the club-face is square at impact.

Playing in the wind

It is often said that the wind "separates the men from the boys." It also separates the good golfer from the bad one. Nothing is easier than to crack up when the wind starts to blow. You need to think more, and this is the appeal of this kind of weather.

To play well in the wind you need to do the following:

– prepare yourself mentally and look on it with a positive attitude;

– check the direction and strength of the wind. Look at a stretch of water – if it is calm, the wind is blowing from behind; if there are small waves, you are against the wind;

– if you have a choice of balls, it is better to use a two-piece ball;

– lower your grip so that the wind has less effect on the ball;

– position the ball nearer your right foot to create a low trajectory;

– take an extra club, or even two or three more, so

OBSTACLE: GO OVER IT

You have to avoid an obstacle – a bunker or a tree – and you don't know how to go about it. It is relatively simple, if you stick to the following conditions: first, you need a good lie. Next, take a sand wedge, open the face with the blade pointing upward and the sole on the ground. Widen your stance and open it up, with the ball near the left foot. To hit a successful shot, don't be afraid to hit hard, or else the ball will die a few yards from the bunker or tree. The ball rises and stops in proportion to the cleanness of the strike.

TAKE YOUR DRIVER

You have to play a shot which requires a long iron. You risk hitting short, as the green is over 200 yards away (180 m). Why not use a driver? Shorten your grip, and use a three-quarter swing. Apply yourself. The shot with the driver will give you a long ball which is low and has a good chance of reaching its destination.

that nothing will hinder your ability to maintain a smooth rhythm;

– widen your stance when putting;

– play a 3 wood rather than a driver;

– push the tee into the ground a little more than usual;

– be determined, and don't forget that you are not the only one affected by bad conditions when the wind blows.

The best shot to play in the wind is the draw. You need to align your shoulders and feet to the right of the target, with the clubface pointing toward it.

When the wind is blowing from left to right, the simplest thing is to aim a little to the left and, conversely, when the wind is blowing from right to left, you should aim more to the right.

When the wind is blowing from behind, the danger is to hit the ball too hard, not complete the swing and be in front of the ball during the downswing.

With approach shots into the wind, backspin will be increased. So it is best to use a less open club.

As regards the short game, if the wind is favourable, you need to lift the ball so that it falls to the ground "dead," completely motionless and without rolling. To do this, the ball needs to be near the left foot, with the weight on the left side and use a slow swing.

In a headwind, shorten the swing, with the ball nearer the right foot.

Playing a high ball

There are situations where it is impossible to play anything except a high ball. So prepare yourself in advance. Even on the fairway, you may be led to play a high ball because of a tree situated between you and the green, for example. Before making your shot, try to visualize the type of shot you should play. The rest will happen almost naturally. The aim is to lift the ball into the air quickly. To achieve this, the ball should be near the left foot in the address position, with the weight more on the right foot, and the right shoulder lower than the left one. The left arm leads the swing during the backswing. The openness of the club will do the rest. If the hazard is more than 55 yards (50 m) away, you can use a less lofted club. Your set up position will lift the ball equally well. Trust the loft of your club.

THE PUNCHED SHOT ▶

Your ball is 100 yards (80 m) from the green, with a tree to get past, then a bunker, after which you need to stop the ball at once. Interesting, isn't it? But if the ball is not buried in thick rough, you can play your 9 iron, or your pitching wedge or sand wedge. The ball should be positioned to the right. The weight will tend to be on the left, and will remain there throughout the swing. To give the ball backspin, concentrate on hitting it crisply – the loft of the club will do the rest.

USE A LONG IRON

If you think you can reach the green with a long iron, you should prepare as follows: ball to the right, hands in front of the club. This position will produce a low, soaring ball. At impact the hands should finish low.

SLOPING LIES

When your feet are on a slope, you are never quite sure what to do. The important thing is keep good balance. Rather than overburdening your mind, just remember two things: for an uphill lie, your hips need to be at practically the same level, so you need to bend your left knee. For a downhill lie, the reverse applies. In the set up position, the ball should always be positioned close to the higher foot – the left for an uphill lie, right for a downhill lie.

Playing a low ball

Imagine that your ball is not far from the green, with a tree which is too high to have any hope of hitting over it. The only answer is to hit the ball under the branches. Here again, you need to hit a punched shot, where the ball hardly rises. To do this, address the ball with it slightly to the right of your stance, and position your hands in front. The clubface should be square. The backswing will be short, and the ball is contacted directly. There is absolutely no reason to cock the wrists.

Playing from bare ground

While the professional golfer likes to play a ball from a piece of bare ground because he can give it a lot of backspin, the amateur is not so appreciative, as he does not usually hit the ball cleanly. But the following is what has to be done, or else the club will bounce off. This is particularly true for the sand wedge, which has a wide sole. To decrease this risk, use a pitching wedge or a 9 iron instead. To be sure of making direct contact with the ball, position it near to your right foot, with a slightly open stance. You could also use a putter if the surface is

FLAG AT THE END OF THE GREEN

When the flag is on the second tier of a green, i.e. on the raised area, it is important to get the ball up on to the right level. The critical aspect, however, is not to let the ball roll too much afterward. Using an 8 or 9 iron, with your hands slightly in front of the club, play a relaxed shot, concentrating on accelerating during the downswing.

ROUGH: PLAY WITH THE TOE

If your ball is in the rough near the green, position your sand wedge so that the ball is in contact with the toe of the club. This enables the ball to rise more quickly. The clubface will remain open at impact, which is essential if the grass is high.

sufficiently smooth between you and the green. This technique is called the "Texas wedge."

The ball in a divot

Following the feeling of injustice one gets after hitting a good shot into such a place, you need to act. Forget your wood or long iron. If the ball is plugged in a divot, you will need a 9 iron or even a wedge. In any case, you will have to play a punched shot, i.e. a three-quarters shot, with scarcely any follow-through.

The ball will keep low, and roll a lot. To play this shot, if the divot is not too big, use up to a 6 iron, address the ball in the middle of your stance with your hands in front of the ball, and use an upright backswing. The ball is contacted first. If the ball is actually against the clod of earth, you should cock your wrists even more quickly and hit the earth first.

An obstacle in close proximity

Bushes

Courses that wind their way through a forest are often very beautiful and a great pleasure to play on. All the same, they are usually full of trees and sometimes rocks, and other hidden hazards. When your ball comes down in these areas, you need to negotiate the situation carefully. If it is next to a bush, for example, go into the bush itself if necessary, to get yourself as far from the ball as possible. Adopt a wider stance, with body weight on the left. Grip tightly and lower down the shaft. Cock your wrists quickly during the backswing and make direct contact with the ball. Keep your eyes on the ball all the time.

Rocks or mounds

If your ball is lying less than a yard from a rock, you will find it hard to lift the club normally. Do some practice swings, close the clubface, choosing as open a club as possible, with a low grip, weight on the left and the ball toward the right foot, as in the situation above. Cock your wrists.

Now imagine that there is a mound between your ball and the green, with very little space to get the ball on the green, as the flag is near the edge. There are two possibilities: either to use this mound and hope that the ball will roll toward the flag – risky; or to play a safe shot and lob the ball, even if it means that the ball doesn't finish particularly close to the flag.

TO BE ABLE TO PLAY WELL OFF BARE GROUND, AS GREG NORMAN IS DOING HERE, IS NOT WITHIN THE REACH OF EVERY PLAYER. ONE OF THE SECRETS IS TO PINCH THE BALL, MAKING CONTACT WITH IT BEFORE YOU TOUCH THE GROUND.

107

CHIPPING

Your ball is near the green, on the edge of the rough. Use a sand wedge and play the shot like a putt.

The ball should be slightly toward the right foot. You need to play a rhythmic shot, and have a low backswing as if putting. Hit the ball using your shoulders and arms and not your wrists.

THICK ROUGH: KEEP UPRIGHT

To have any chance of getting out of thick rough, you must do at least one thing: keep the swing arc upright. If it is too flat, the clubface will be held back by the grass. The aim is to make contact with the ball without having any grass in between. The clubface is open and so is the stance, and the swing is carried out mainly with the arms.

THICK ROUGH: TIGHT GRIP

When the ball is lying in high, thick grass, you shouldn't just grit your teeth, but grip the club so that it doesn't wobble upon impact and prevent the face closing again. The speed of the swing should be the same for the backswing and downswing.

BARE GROUND: ATTACK THE BALL

The greatest champions, like the American Tom Watson, believe that a ball lying on a road, for example, is not as difficult to play as people often think, provided you make contact with it first.

The ball should be toward the right foot, with your hands in front of the club and the body weight on the left. It is advisable to use a pitching wedge rather than a sand wedge, whose wide sole may rebound off the bare ground, while the pitching wedge will slide under the ball better.

CHIP WITH A WOOD

Occasionally exceptional methods are called for in exceptional circumstances. When you are in the rough on the edge of the green, here is a useful tip which often works: use a wood, which you play as if you had a heavy putter in your hand. The idea may seem strange, but think about it. The head of the wood is easier to slide through the grass than an iron, especially when the rough is very thick.

When the ball is higher than your feet

The mere fact that the ball is not at the same level as the feet often strips a player of all good sense. You only need to think for a little while to work out what you need to do:
– get near the ball;
– take time to assess the situation;
– hold the club further down the shaft;
– flex your knees slightly when addressing the ball and straighten your chest a little;
– keep your weight on your toes;
– use a longer club;
– aim a little to the right as the slope will naturally draw the shot to the left;

Swing compactly, but without strain. If the slope is really severe, shorten your pivot, otherwise you risk losing your balance. Hit the shot more with your hands and arms.

When the ball is lower than your feet

This is the opposite situation. Is it easier or not? Perhaps it is. In any case, this kind of shot is not

WHEN THE LIE IS UPHILL, DON'T PANIC. ON THE CONTRARY, YOU SHOULD DRAW ON YOUR RESOURCES, SHORTEN THE MOVEMENT AND PLAY CONFIDENTLY LIKE MARK MCNULTY DOES HERE TO GET OUT OF A PARTICULARLY TRICKY BUNKER.

insurmountable provided the correct technique is used. When the ball is lower than your feet, you should:
– get close to the ball;
– stand in the set up position to the left to counteract the ball's natural tendency to go to the left;
– flex your knees normally;
– weight more on your heels;
– use a longer club;
– swing compactly and rhythmically.

If the slope is steep, play even more slowly, don't attempt to turn too much, swing with your arms first. It is important to keep your balance.

An uphill lie

An uphill lie means that your left foot is higher than your right foot. The situation is therefore different from the one where the ball is higher than your feet. You need to adapt as follows:
– in the set up position, your weight is more on the right (not all the experts agree on this);
– the ball is positioned near to the left foot, but not too near;
– the club used should be less lofted than normal, as the trajectory of the ball will be higher;

– aim to the right to avoid playing a pull (entirely to the left);
– your wrists should remain firm and the finish should be short.

Take care! You must concentrate on keeping close to the ground in the backswing.

The downhill lie

Here, the right foot is higher than the left, and so the situation is reversed.
– in the set up position, the weight is on the left;
– the ball is positioned near to the right foot, but not too close;
– the club used is more lofted, as the trajectory will be lower;
– aim to the left to avoid a push (entirely to the right);
– the swing should be more upright but the finish will be high.

Whether it is an uphill or downhill lie, it is definitely not advisable to use a wood. The important thing is to get out of this bad patch and think of getting as much distance as possible.

The last and most complex case is when the lie is downhill with a side slope. Remember the principles listed for the ball being below your feet.

◀ BACK TO THE FLAG

If your ball is lying near a tree and is impossible to play normally, there are two possible solutions: either to play left-handed, with the other side of the clubface, which is not as hard as you might imagine, or to play with your back to the hole, i.e. not looking at the target when you hit the ball. If you choose the second solution, you only need a little skill to make a successful shot. Take the club in one hand (right hand) if you are right-handed, preferably a 9 iron or a wedge. With practice, this shot will become easier.

GO ROUND THE OBSTACLE

Your ball is behind a tree which is blocking the path to the green. There is the possibility of going round the obstacle by imparting spin to your ball. For example, the green is to the left of the tree. A right-to-left shot is required. To carry this out, close the clubface and use your normal grip. Your stance should also be normal, with the ball toward the right foot. Aim at the right side of the tree you wish to go round, and hit. The ball should go to the right then come back in to the left, rolling slightly.

THE SHORT GAME

This is an area of the game where a player needs to be able to "feel" the situation. It requires a long apprenticeship and a great deal of experience. It is often said that naturally gifted players have most success in this department of the game, but then their talent is often explained by a frightening amount of hard work, plus an understanding of all the possible situations. And heaven knows, there are enough of them!

For the beginner or average player, the short game is the best way of salvaging the scorecard, but it is not free from its problems. You need endless hours of practice before you can start to feel good about it.

If we wanted to sum up the main types of shot, or the approaches to the short game, we could say that broadly speaking there are two dominant methods. The first involves the "triangle" theory, which forbids using the wrists, while the other demands a pronounced hand and wrist action. At club level, there are those who favor much use of the pitching wedge and those who prefer using the chipper. The pitching wedge gives the ball a high trajectory with little roll, and the chipper achieves more distance.

Each theory has its advantages and disadvantages. But we won't get involved in this ancient debate, rather we will concentrate on the two ways of playing shots around the green. You must judge for yourself on the basis of your own

THE SHORT GAME IS THE
BEST WAY OF SALVAGING
YOUR SCORE, PROVIDED
YOU WORK HARD AT THIS
ASPECT OF THE GAME.
YOU ONLY ACQUIRE
TOUCH OR "FEEL" AFTER
A GREAT DEAL OF
PRACTICE.

THINK OF THE TIME

It is important, but not easy, to be able to hit shots with the wedge at half, and not full, power. Here is a useful tip to help you to do this: practice lifting your club to a position corresponding to 10 o'clock on a clock face. Then swing down, accelerating normally and measure the average distance your ball travels – let's say 55 yards (50 m). This will act as a marker. If you don't want to hit the ball so far, lift your hands to 8 or 9 o'clock. If you want to hit it further, lift your club to 11 o'clock.

PUTT BY CHIPPING

To achieve a consistent chip from the edge of the green, try this method. You will hit a low shot, without cocking your wrists. Remember to follow-through well after impact. The only adjustment to make is in terms of the ball position, which should be toward the right foot for a low shot, and to the left for a higher trajectory. Clearly, the greatest difficulty is in gauging the shot accurately, but after a bit of practice, you will get the ball near the hole more often.

HANDS CROSS THE LINE FIRST

There is nothing worse than watching players cock their wrists with the club ahead at impact in the hope of making the ball rise. You should really do quite the opposite. Think of a thread going from your chin to the ball. Your hands should cut this thread during the downswing. This will make your shots more assured, and will increase your chances of getting near the flag.

CLOSED CLUB ON THE EDGE OF THE GREEN ▶

Contrary to popular belief, it is not recommended to use a very lofted club when the ball is on the edge of the green, say about 4 feet (1.2 m) from the putting surface. You should in fact use a closed club, a 5 or 6 iron. It depends on the lie, and on the confidence you have in a particular club, and also on the distance in relation to the hole. If the ball is further away, say between 2 and 5 yards (2–5 m) from the green, use a 7 or an 8 iron instead.

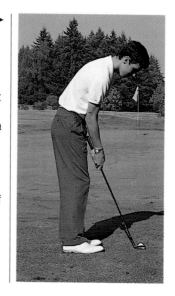

IT IS IMPORTANT TO LEARN HOW TO GET OUT OF BAD SITUATIONS. YOU NEED TO KNOW WHAT TACTICS TO ADOPT AND WHICH IS THE CORRECT CLUB TO USE. YOU SHOULD MANAGE WITH A BIT OF LUCK!

experience. The first thing to realize is that a different shot is required for every situation.

But before going into details, it is vital to use the same routine before playing. It will help you to win matches.

A golf game is won on technical merits, but it is also won on the mental level. It is very important to have a clear idea of the shot required. To do so, you need to examine the situation carefully. Should you play a high, low or medium-height shot? Once you have decided, choose an exact point where you want the ball to land. Think about the green, its slopes and contours. Then try to imagine the trajectory and roll of the ball. Before you play a short shot, always go to the spot where your ball should land to check that there is no problem with the surface, for example, that there is no clod or mound of earth from which the ball might rebound. Do a practice swing to memorize the shot you are going to play and retain your feel for the stroke.

This entire procedure should be automatic, and should not slow down the game. It is easy to understand why players like Jack Nicklaus, Nick Faldo and Bernhard Langer take so many precautions – but it is usually worth the effort.

The short game is often neglected in practice.

THE RIGHT KNEE

To be able to chip successfully, think of sliding your right knee toward your left knee during the downswing and of lifting your right foot. This does not mean that your whole body should move. On the other hand, you need to remain relatively upright, but allow your legs to move slightly.

OPEN YOUR STANCE

To make your chip shot more accurate, open your stance. Cock your wrists during the backswing, but keep them locked at impact.

THE HEEL FIRST

In order to prevent your right hand action from being too pronounced during the downswing, before you play your chip shot imagine that the heel of the club is leading. In this way, its toe will not get ahead of the heel. The left side should stay strong, and the left wrist should not be cocked.

SYMMETRY

Approach shots often fail because club speed slows at impact. To put this right, lift the club to waist height only and follow-through to waist height.

LEAN TO THE LEFT ▶

All approach shots should be hit coming down. To get the club to touch the ball before it hits the ground, lean slightly to the left when addressing the ball and stay like this while you are playing the shot. The weight will remain mostly on the left and you will get a more upright swing arc. It will be a case of "ball-to-ground" rather than "ground-to-ball." To hit the ball cleanly, place five balls 4 inches (10 cm) in front of the ball to be hit. If you make contact with them, your swing is not upright enough.

LESS PRESSURE ON THE GRIP

When you want to play a lobbed shot from the rough around the green, for example, you should use a light grip, and let the sand wedge do the work. Because of its weight and loft, it gets through the turf well.

A BUCKET FOR ACCURACY

Take advantage of your garden to practice the short game. Position a bucket a short distance away with an obstacle between yourself and the bucket, say a bench or child's swing. The exercise consists of getting the ball into the bucket through the obstacle.

◀ OVER THE BUNKER

To play this kind of shot, it is advisable to take a step back from the ball, widen your stance, flex your knees more and above all brace your right leg, turning the knee outward. The swing arc will be less upright, but do not strain to create a flatter swing plane. The position adopted, with your weight on the right, should make the movement happen naturally.

LOWER YOUR GRIP ▶

For short shots, it is often a good idea to adopt a lower or shorter grip on the shaft. You should also keep the same grip regardless of the club used or you will never have the same feeling twice. One more thing to remember: if you decide to use a shorter grip, you will need to hit the ball harder to achieve the same distance.

WATCH OUT FOR BACKSPIN!

Backspin is fine, most of the time, but it can be dangerous. If the shot is not well executed, the ball can be thinned and go at quite dramatic speed. Some experts do not recommend it because it is difficult and needs a lot of practice. Nevertheless, for experienced players, it adds another shot to their repertoire.

PRACTICE CLUB ▶

For the chip shot, it is important to have the feeling of keeping your wrists firm. A good test of this is to make a model club yourself. Take the grip of an old club, and add an old shaft taken from another club. The two shafts should be joined to make an extended club measuring 2 yards (2 m). Now play. You will notice that your left arm stays close to your body, and that your wrists are firm. If you use your wrists too much, the shaft will hit your ribs and you will soon get the idea!

PLAY ON THE OUTSIDE

To effect a takeaway on the outside in relation to the target line, make the clubhead move outward in relation to the hands throughout the swing. The rest of the swing should be carried out normally. After impact, the club should point outward and upward again.

PRECEDING PAGES:
THE SUPERB FORÊT
DES LANDES LENDS
BEAUTY TO THE
LANDSCAPE AT
MOLIETS. THIS LONG
AND UNDULATING
COURSE RUNS
BETWEEN THE SEA AND
THE FOREST.

FACING PAGE:
THE BASIC PRINCIPLES
ARE THE SAME,
WHETHER YOU DECIDE
TO USE A PITCHING
WEDGE OR A CHIPPER.
HOWEVER, THE SWING
IS NARROWER FOR THE
CHIP SHOT.

This is frequently due to a lack of adequate practice facilities, but sometimes it is due to a casual attitude. This is a great shame, as good putting is dependent on a good short game.

So, there are two ways of playing shots: hitting the high ball with the pitching wedge, or hitting a low ball with a chipper (the chip shot, or chip-and-run, as it is known).

The pitching wedge

The openness of the club will lift the ball, without you needing to "help" it up. However, the left arm has to work, while the right arm remains passive.

What makes the ball rise so quickly?

It is merely the movement of the club coming downward on impact. The hands should be in front in relation to the ball, with the weight on the left.

What should you do if you want to hit the ball higher or lower?

You simply modify your set up position. To hit a ball of average height, if your feet are aligned on the left of the target, your shoulders and clubface are square. If you don't want to hit the ball too high, it is sufficient to open the clubface and align your body slightly to the left of the target. The swing itself does not change. The ball has every chance of dropping gently when it lands. These adjustments vary the height of the ball.

Other important elements in hitting a successful pitch shot include good rhythm, and being able to vary the width of the swing according to the distance to be covered.

One last piece of advice: don't try to "scoop" the ball under any circumstances. It is not necessary. You should start the swing by cocking your left wrist in order to lift the club quickly, and by bending your right elbow, trying not to move the body – especially the lower half.

The chip shot

You will often play a chip shot when there is a distance of 25 yards (20 m) or less between the ball and the pin. If the distance is greater, it is usually best to use a pitching wedge.

You can also play a chip shot when the wind is unfavorable, to avoid the ball being carried adrift. The chip shot is also used when there is a hazard to be avoided between the ball and the green. If the green has two levels it is best

◄ FORGET THE TARGET

To stop raising your head during the backswing, practice keeping your eyes fixed on where the ball is positioned, even after it has left the ground. Don't look where it has gone. Concentrate on the ball first, then work on distance.

LIFT YOUR RIGHT HEEL

To avoid fluffing or topping the ball, concentrate on keeping your hands in front at the address position, and on lifting the right heel during the downswing, with your bodyweight on the left side. At impact, lean on your right toe to keep perfect balance.

THE PENDULUM ►

The pendulum method is not used just for putting. It is also useful for the chip shot when the lie is bad, i.e. on bare ground. If the clubface is open, the club will slide along the ground. In this case, you need to use a sand wedge with a square stance, keeping your feet a normal distance apart. The ball is in the center of the stance, and the hands form an extension of the club. The grip is firm and your arms and shoulders rise like a pendulum without cocking your wrists. You hit the ball at the lowest point of the swing

arc. The body stays still.

AN INTERMEDIATE TARGET

If you have a short chip shot to play onto the green, the best thing to do after analyzing the lie is to find an intermediate target toward which the ball will roll before heading toward the hole. Aim at this target and hit the ball toward it.

A CONTRACTED STANCE

The shorter the swing, the narrower the stance should be. If you are on the edge of the green, your feet should be almost touching each other.

THE SAME TARGET USING DIFFERENT CLUBS

You may wonder how to assess the likely distance that the ball will travel when it is hit with clubs as different as the sand wedge and the 9, 7 or 5 iron. It's fairly simple. Decide on an intermediate target for all these clubs and then stick to it. You will then see the difference between each one, and which goes furthest.

MAKE THE HOLE BIGGER

When you are practicing, it is important to visualize yourself actually playing on the course. A good exercise consists of imagining that there is a concentric circle of about a yard (1 m) in diameter surrounding the hole; try to get every ball you hit inside it. If you manage to get three-quarters of the balls in, you are certainly on your way to becoming a good approach shot player.

THE TRIANGLE

If you want to make the ball run, don't get into a swing position which will put backspin on it.

Think in terms of the swing forming a triangle. Start off with your shoulders, arms and hands all moving together in a single movement. Use a 7 iron and strike the ball firmly – it will have very little spin on it and will roll two-thirds of the distance. Don't cock your wrists when you follow-through.

CROSS YOUR LEGS ►

How many times have you seen golfers transferring their body weight during the backswing and staying in that position during the downswing! You can guess the result. To hit a good chip shot, practice crossing your legs, with the right in front of the left which is slightly bent. You will have no choice but to keep your weight on the left.

to use a medium iron and play a chip shot, unless it is wet.

Which club should you use?

There is a wide range of possibilities, from a 5 iron to a 9 iron. In general, the ideal club is the 7 iron. It is better than a 9 iron because the trajectory is lower, and it is easier to assess roll.

There is less risk of hitting a bad shot than there is with a 9 iron.

How do you play a chip shot?

In the classic chip shot, the feet, hips and knees are open. The weight is on the left, and the hands are slightly in front of the ball. The aim is to get the minimum lift on the ball. To do this, keep the club close to the ground and raise it comparatively little, as if you were taking back your putter. Keep your left wrist firm just after impact. The swing takes place by virtue of the shoulder and arm action, with scarcely any wrist action, as if the hands were in plaster. A wristy, jerky action is often explained by a lack of confidence in one's ability to lift the ball.

To succeed with a chip shot, you must not use your wrists but you must keep your hands in front of the clubhead at impact. During the backswing, the right wrist is naturally cocked. To increase accuracy, extend your arms at impact and point the club at the target. Your knees should be slightly bent and directed toward the target too. Although medium irons are usually best for chip shots, under certain circumstances you can use a wedge or even a sand wedge. The main prerequisite is to have a good lie. The shot is lobbed, and played with an open stance, a square clubface and with the ball positioned toward the left foot. A slightly shortened backswing is required, together with a slow, regular rhythm.

Golf presents many unusual situations. The best solution is to adapt to them … technique is not always enough!

THE BRITISH PLAYER LAURA DAVIES IS CURRENTLY THE WORLD'S NUMBER ONE WOMAN GOLFER, RIVAL OF MARIE-LAURE DE LORENZI. SHE HAS EXTRAORDINARY POWER, A VERY NATURAL GAME AND A RARE TOUCH.

119

THE SHORT GAME

◄ FLUFFING: HANDS IN FRONT

If you tend to fluff the ball when playing chip shots, position your hands in front of the ball. Try not to force the ball up – the loft of the club will do it for you.

PLAY IN THE SAME PLACE USING DIFFERENT CLUBS

To find out which club to use, try the following test. Play a chip shot with different clubs, aiming at the same target and hit each ball with the same amount of power. You will see how the different clubs react to the same shot.

A MORE CLOSED CLUB FOR RAISED GREENS

Imagine your ball is about 50 yards (45 m) from the green. You decide to use a sand wedge. You hit a solid shot and the ball rises and pitches about 10 yards (10 m) from the pin. But it stops quickly, a bit short. If you had used a pitching wedge, the ball would have gone lower and rolled more, finishing nearer to the pin. You wouldn't have had to worry about taking three putts to get it in!

COPY YOUR FIRST BALL

A good way of visualizing the trajectory of your approach shot is to play two balls when practicing. Play the first and watch its trajectory, provided the shot is a good one. Remember the path of the first ball when you hit the second. You will be amazed to see how little difference there is between them.

BUNKERS

Landing in a bunker can be both the best and worst thing that can happen to a golfer. In general, the professional golfer has no fear of bunkers, but most weekend golfers are terrified of these sandy hollows which punctuate the course. They shouldn't be. What he or she doesn't realize is that getting out of a bunker is often a relatively easy shot, provided the player has a good understanding of the technique required.

In fact, technology has developed so much in the last fifty years that some professionals, including Tom Watson, have criticized the situation, arguing that it levels standards too much. This might be true for professionals, but, let's face it, we poor amateurs would be lost if we didn't have a sand wedge in our bags! Imagine if we had to play with the old niblicks that our grandparents used. In addition to this, for various reasons, getting out of a bunker is often the aspect of the game which is most neglected by players when they practice. Golf clubs are partly at fault, as facilities do not usually include practice bunkers. Also, golfers prefer to practice their long game or putting, and do not devote nearly enough time to improving their short games.

Technique

Before examining the necessary skills required for getting out of bunkers, attention should be drawn

CONTRARY TO POPULAR BELIEF, GETTING OUT OF A BUNKER IS NOT AS HARD AS IT LOOKS. IT IS SPECTACULAR, AS THIS PHOTO SHOWS.

to one very important point: getting out of a bunker is not difficult in itself, and is in fact easier than an approach shot because one has the advantage of a greater margin of error, provided the ball is not hit too hard. That is the crux of the matter. If you try to hit the ball too hard, the club will dig into the sand or will move out of a good plane. In both cases, the ball may well stay in the bunker.

Take your sand wedge, anchor your feet firmly in the sand and open the clubface – do not rest it on the sand, as this is forbidden. Now, open your stance, i.e. position your body to the left of the target. Use your normal swing. This very specific set up position creates an outside-to-inside swing plane which will make the ball rise very quickly, the openness of the stance compensating for the orientation to the right. To be certain of having your weight on the left side after impact, shift your weight slightly on the left in the set up position. As regards ball position, this should be in front of the left foot. The grip has not been discussed quite simply because it doesn't change. It is as normal, even though the clubface is open.

If the backswing varies according to the distance to be covered, the swing stays about the same. Try to hit about an inch and a half (4 cm) behind the ball, when playing out of the sand.

Different situations

A bunker close to the green
This shot is not as easy as it looks because you need to judge it very precisely. No one is expecting you to get the ball in the hole, nor even to get it within a yard (1 m) of the pin, just to get it onto the green. To achieve even this, you need to have good feel in your hands and to have practiced. If the bunker is 2 yards (2 m) from the green and just 4 yards (4 m) from the pin, you can play boldly – you risk overshooting but that is better than the ball staying in the bunker. Open the club face a little, and open your stance and body to an equal degree. Take a little more sand, and relax.

A bunker that is not adjacent to the green
Let's say it is a fairway bunker situated 35 yards (30 m) from the green. If the bunker is not too deep, use an 8 iron, and not a sand wedge.

If it's a fairway bunker about 100 or so yards (about 100 m) from the green, use a 6 or 7 iron and open the clubface a little more than usual, the same applies to your stance and your body alignment in relation to the target.

Use a firm grip, don't make a complete back-

WITHOUT THE BALL

It is easy to forget that it is the sand which makes the ball move and which carries it. To get the feel of this, try this simple tip: practice in the sand without the ball. Simply hit down into the sand and be sure to complete your follow-through. There is nothing more dangerous than leaving the clubhead buried in the sand just because you are afraid of following through, in the false belief that the ball will go too far.

WHEN TO FORGET THE EXPLOSION

You can still get out of a greenside bunker with a pitching wedge if you want the ball to go lower. This is only possible, however, if the lip is not too severe. You might even consider a chip shot from the sand.

There is one prerequisite for success: hit the ball before the sand. To practice this, take a flat piece of wood and practice hitting the ball first. If you don't hit the ball first, you will notice that the clubhead bounces off the wood, and you will hit a bad shot.

OVER THE BUNKER

The shot played toward the green over a bunker is not easy, and is often intimidating. To play this shot, lock your right leg in the set up position, pointing the right knee to the outside. This will help you to keep your weight on the right side during the downswing. Use your wedge or sand wedge and open the clubface. Follow through well, without trying to hit hard.

A SAND CAKE

It is difficult to imagine practicing in a bunker without a ball. However, it is an excellent way of seeing how the club works in the sand.

Imagine a circle the size of a cake, about 4 inches (10 cm) in diameter. Plant your feet firmly into the sand. The idea is to send the whole cake flying. Try it, checking the size of the divot you send into the air. Then take a ball and do the same thing, again trying to lift up the area surrounding the ball.

swing but transfer your weight well during the downswing. There is clearly no need to take any sand. You should make contact with the ball directly.

If it is in a bunker 150 yards (150 m) from the green, use the same technique as above but consider the following alternative: if the bunker is shallow, you could use a fairway wood. But take care – it's not always worth taking the risk! The lie should be perfect if you are going to use a wood. If you are in the slightest doubt, use a 4 or 5 iron.

Your feet are below the ball

Don't change your posture, but modify your grip by shortening it. Position yourself more to the right, as the ball will tend to go to the left. Position the ball nearer the right foot. Don't forget to anchor your feet well into the sand, but not excessively, or you will be too low down in relation to the ball. Don't take a full backswing.

Your feet are above the ball

Not a very nice position! Above all, don't flex your knees too much, but lean from the pelvis to keep a wide swing. It is also very important to aim more to the left.

The ball is in the bunker, but your feet are outside the hazard

This situation is particularly tricky to deal with. It all depends on the depth of the bunker, but whatever that may be, widen your stance slightly, hold the club firmly at the end of the shaft and lean forward from the pelvis to lower your shoulders in the address position. The ball is played in the center. Use a fairly slow swing, or else you may lose your balance. Remember to keep your head down and don't be afraid to take plenty of sand.

A downhill lie

It is important to stay well balanced and follow the slope. If your upper body slides toward the target, you might top the ball. To be stable during the swing, keep your weight on the left and flex your knees in the set up position. Your stance should be open, with the ball in the middle of your feet. The club rises quickly and your wrists are cocked. The swing plane must be outside-to-inside.

The club should take up a little sand but be careful, this is a difficult shot. Exactly! Just relax and take a few more moments to plan your stroke.

If the lie is uphill, do the reverse.

LEADING AMATEUR PLAYER, PETER MCEVOY. HERE WE SEE HIM COMING OUT OF A BUNKER WITH IMPECCABLE STYLE. HOW EASY GOLF CAN SEEM WHEN EVERYTHING GOES RIGHT!

124

BUNKERS

A SOUP BOWL OR A TEACUP

It all depends on the distance you have to cover to reach the pin. If it is a long way, say, over 5 yards (5 m), you shouldn't take too much sand. Think of a soup bowl. If the distance is less than 5 yards (5 m), have a mental picture of a teacup, hitting the shot coming down, with a very upright swing arc.

HIT A SAND DIVOT

Draw two horizontal lines in the sand, one 2 inches (5 cm) in front of the ball and the other 2 inches (5 cm) behind it. Practice hitting a sand divot, playing between these two lines. You will soon get the feeling of an explosion, which is what you need to get out of a bunker.

ADJUST YOUR STANCE

It is often thought that the length of a shot depends solely on the width of the swing arc or on the force with which the shot is hit. Stance counts for something too. If you only need to cover a short distance to get out of a bunker, position the ball near the left foot. If it is further, position the ball nearer the center. Why? Because the further to the left that the ball is, the more sand there is between the club and the ball. Your shot will therefore be short.

A LONG WAY OUT

If you have to cover a distance of 10 to 25 yards (10–25 m) before reaching the green, you will be facing a very difficult shot. To achieve the necessary distance, you may need to use a club which is less lofted than the sand wedge, a wedge or 9 iron, for example, if the bunker is not too sloping. At the moment of impact, close the clubface. The ball will go further.

WHEN THE BALL IS LYING IN A RUT OR FOOTPRINTS

One of the most terrifying shots in golf – although it is still possible to recover. Tom Watson advises passing the lower edge of the clubhead just under the ball. If the ball is easily accessible from behind, open the blade with an upright swing. On the other hand, if the ball is buried with a lot of sand behind it, close the blade.

The ball is up against the face of the bunker
This shot is totally unfair! However, it has to be dealt with, like all the others. It goes without saying that the aim is not to get the ball in the hole, but simply to get the ball out of the bunker. It is important to get the ball to climb right from the start, and to do this, the face of your sand wedge should be as open as possible. As you are virtually off balance with your left foot, which is higher than the right one, you must keep the lower body still.

Another vital point: you should hug the lie of the land and keep your right shoulder lower than your left in the set up position. If not, you risk sending the ball deeper into the sand with no hope of getting it out again. Lock your swing after impact or else you may hurt your wrists.

The plugged ball
If by misfortune your ball is plugged in its own pitchmark, probably because the sand is very soft, or if it is in a footprint, don't expect a miracle when you try to get it out.

Your stance is normal, the ball is in the middle of your feet and above all, the clubface is quite closed owing to the volume of sand that you will take. Scooping up sand will make the face

SQUARE FOR LONG SHOTS

When the bunker is close to the green, the clubface is open, and your feet and body are aligned on the left of the target. To get out of a bunker further away, everything should be square, i.e. aligned perpendicularly with the target line.

The stance is only slightly more open, the arms can move more freely and the swing is wider. The ball will go further. And the club will cut into the sand less than for a "normal" shot out of the bunker.

THREE BALLS IN A BUNKER ▶

To understand where the club should cut into the sand, put three balls side by side aligned with the pin and play normally. This exercise, which should be repeated, helps to improve alignment and acceleration. The first ball will rise sharply, the other two less so: the distance will be the same.

TO STOP THE BALL

The pin is just 2 yards (2 m) above you but you have an enormous Scottish links style bunker to negotiate. What should you do? Open the clubface and use a light grip with your hands turned to the left. The ball should be toward your left foot, and your hands already behind the clubhead. At impact, the club will be ahead, or else you risk shanking, and your weight will remain mostly on the right. If the clubface is very open, the club will not go too far into the sand and you will produce a lobbed shot which will stop quickly.

126

CLUB ABOVE THE BALL

By advising players to take plenty of sand to avoid topping the ball, it often happens that the player digs his club too far into the sand and the ball stays there. To avoid this, address the ball so that the club is above it, and actually hides it. Keep an upright swing.

GETTING OUT WITH ONE HAND ►

To show how relatively easy it is to get out of a bunker, coaches often play with one hand only, i.e. their right hand.

Try playing with one hand yourself. It will give you confidence.

CUT THE TEE IN HALF ►

If you find it hard to imagine the ideal shot, put a tee in the sand with just the top sticking out. Then play a shot, trying to break the tee in half. You will go under the ball better and will follow through correctly.

BUNKERS: LOOK AT YOUR FOOTPRINTS

If the tracks are deep, the sand will be soft and compacted. You must open the clubface more and accelerate the speed of the club to avoid it digging too deeply into the sand. The reverse is true if the sand is light.

become square again upon impact. The backswing should be upright to lift the ball as quickly as possible. You should never strike the ball first, always catch the sand first. The more you scoop up, the further the ball will roll. This type of shot is faced quite frequently. It is important to know how to play it. Practice!

Errors to avoid

Nothing resembles one bunker more than another bunker. Yet each one is different and should be played in a particular way.

The first mistake is to hit the ball too clearly without catching any sand. The ball shoots over the green.

Then there is the straightforward topped shot. Once again, there is no question of finding the ball on the green, indeed, it may even be lost forever.

The third error is when the ball hardly moves at all.

These three mistakes all have an explanation: in the first two cases, it may be a set up problem (for example, the ball was positioned too far to the right, hence the club made contact with it too soon, without hitting the sand). In the third case, the ball stays in the sand because the club did not get through the sand properly.

But the major cause of a ball going off like a rocket is having too wide a swing arc with an angle of attack which is too flat. Slowing down at impact implies a bad grip or feet too deeply anchored into the ground.

There are, in fact, thousands of explanations for these types of mistake.

CURTIS STRANGE, ONE OF THOSE FORTUNATE PEOPLE TO WHOM A BUNKER PRESENTS NO REAL OBSTACLE.

HANDS IN THE SAND ▶

Too many average golfers relax their hands at the moment of impact. It is not enough to have the correct stance, an upright backswing and to be able to control the downswing. If your hands don't "follow" the sand after impact, there is little chance of getting out successfully. Think about this every time you try to get out of a bunker: your hands should point toward the target, especially the left hand.

GETTING OUT OF A BUNKER: THE SMART APPROACH

If the sand is wet or very hard, it is often preferable to leave your sand wedge in the bag and try an approach shot?

Use a 7, 8 or 9 iron. But the bunker needs to be fairly shallow, with little or no face to negotiate.

Using your iron, address the ball at the height of your left heel and put your weight on the left side, with your hands ahead of the ball. Keep close to the sand during the backswing, and above all, hit the ball before the sand.

GRIP FIRST

Getting out of a greenside bunker is simple enough if you bear the following in mind. Before going into the bunker, grip the club so that the face of the sand wedge is quite open. Go into the bunker only after you have adopted your grip, and hit the ball out without altering the position of your hands on the club. The ideal grip for this type of shot is the so-called light grip (left hand turned to the right). It will prevent your hands from closing the clubface, which would cause you to take too much sand and to stop the swing too quickly.

ANCHORAGE

Your ball is in a fairway bunker. You should use a medium iron or even a long iron if you need it to reach the green in two shots. The first thing to do in this case is to anchor your feet firmly on the ground. (It should feel as if your feet are stuck in a block of cement.) Only the upper body should move.

PUTTING

Anyone who has played golf will soon realize that putting is of enormous importance. It wins and loses games. If you consider that you take an average of two putts per hole, then putting represents half of the entire game in itself.

So, you will say, what miracle cure or secret do you recommend to lower my scores? Unfortunately, the reply is "None." If you watch the greatest champions and examine their games in detail you will realize that there is no general rule for success on the greens. For instance, Severiano Ballesteros, Tom Watson, and the Japanese player Isao Aoki have almost nothing in common when they putt. Yet they are all great exponents of putting. Ballesteros' swing is flowing, Watson's is compact, and Aoki's is staccato with a lot of wrist movement.

It has to be said that putting is a game within a game. It requires qualities which are not found in other areas, such as touch and feel, more personal qualities than those needed in the main game.

There are three sorts of putters: the good putter, the inconsistent putter and the bad putter. The good putter adapts his game to any surface – fast or slow, flat or sloping. The inconsistent putter has good days and bad days without ever knowing why he succeeds or fails. The bad putter, (who always has "bad luck") sometimes blames his putter, sometimes the condition of the greens. Most golfers suffer from the frustrations of

PUTTING IS VIRTUALLY HALF THE GAME. IT IS VERY IMPORTANT TO REMEMBER THIS. GAMES ARE WON AND LOST ON THE PUTTING GREEN.

LEFT: THE AMERICAN ANDY NORTH, SURPRISE WINNER OF THE U.S. OPEN, SO TALL THAT HE LOOKS LIKE AN ALBATROSS ON THE GREEN.

FACING PAGE: A YOUNG AMATEUR HOPEFUL, DELPHINE BOURSON. A CLASSIC PUTTING POSITION, STUDYING THE CORRECT LINE OF THE PUTT. THIS IS IMPORTANT, ESPECIALLY ON MODERN, CHURNED UP GREENS.

putting. Yet to be described as "a great putter" is not always taken as a compliment. It implies that the rest of the game is not all it should be.... Putting is often underestimated, and it does not deserve to be.

The basic principles remain the same: aim, grip, ball position, alignment of feet and body, posture. Let's dwell on the grip for a moment. The most commonly used grip is the reverse overlap. The palms of the hand are on each side of the shaft, thumbs at the front. The right hand is placed under the left hand, directly against it. The index finger of the left hand rests on the fingers of the right hand. The major advantage of this grip is that it allows the left hand to stay firm while the stroke is being played.

There are lots of other ways of holding the putter. In one of these, the reverse grip, the right hand is above the left hand. In this way the left arm and hand have better control of the shot. If you are having a putting crisis, you can always try this grip, which also protects you from the dangers of hitting a yipped shot.

To simplify things, there are two major putting swing theories which each have their supporters. There is the pendulum theory, with predominant shoulder and arm action, and the hands and

KEEP YOUR HEAD STILL

There is no foolproof method of putting. At least that's the general opinion. In fact, whether your stance is open or closed, whether you play with the wrists or the forearms, eyes over the ball or behind it, normal or reverse grip, it doesn't really matter in the end. But one thing must be totally adhered to: you must not move your head at any time during the movement. If you move it for a second, the alignment is spoilt, along with your chances of getting the ball into the hole.

A CLUB TO SWEEP THE PATH　▶

To enable you to get round an obstruction. Sometimes greens, especially modern ones, get very churned up. Your three putts are at risk every time. This happens with very sloping greens. It is difficult to memorize these slopes and think of a way of tackling them. Take this tip: practice by laying a club on the ground so that you are obliged to go round it. You will have to aim to the left or right accordingly, and most of all it will teach you to use slopes to the best advantage.

THE GUNSHOT

A useful mental image to help keep your head and eyes fixed on the ball is to imagine you are looking down the barrel of a gun, with a hole at the end of it.

RUNNING WATER

When you have difficulty in reading a green, imagine that the line of the putt is covered in water running along a particular trajectory. Copy the line of the putt, according to the direction of the water.

THE WOODEN PLANK ▶

To refine your alignment and the trajectory you wish to give the ball, lay a plank of wood close to the hole, in front of it. Practice pushing the ball without raising the club. Then use a short backswing. If you find you are wrongly aligned on the left, it is probably because your action was too inside-outside. Now lay the plank outward and parallel to the hole, or conversely, if you are aligned too far to the right. The plank also serves to determine whether the clubface is open or closed.

OPEN SHOULDERS

If your putts all end up to the left of the hole, it's probably because your right hand is too dominant. To avoid this, open your shoulders so that they point left of the hole when addressing the ball. The right side lowers, the right arm is close to the body. Your hands, arms and shoulders all work together during the putt.

FOR IMPROVED IMPACT

One of the most important things to remember in putting is to accelerate before impact. This means shortening the backswing as much as possible. By placing a second ball 4 inches (10 cm) behind the first one, you will have no other choice than to shorten the backswing, and will therefore be obliged to speed up the downswing.

AN INTERMEDIATE HOLE

For putts on a slope, it's a good idea to aim at an imaginary hole between the ball and the actual hole. Think about it.

PRACTICING SHORT PUTTS

The outcome of the game depends on the short putts – of less than 1 yard (1 m). Get into the habit of practicing, i.e. of replaying what should be the last putt, with the prior approval of your playing partners. To feel confident, it is important to practice a great deal beforehand. Above all, when you have a putt less than 1.5 yards (1.5 m) long, don't look for a slope where there isn't one. Play straight to the target – it's the only way to get it in.

LEFT SHOULDER TOO

When people speak of the body moving, they often think of the head. That is quite right, but you shouldn't forget that the rest of you can move too. If you try to keep your left shoulder still, you won't have any more problems, as it controls all the top half of your body.

PUTT ON A SLOPE ▶

If you can't manage to read slopes, tell yourself that you are dealing with a straight putt in all situations. Just adapt yourself to it. If it is a right-to-left slope for example, choose a point to the right of the hole, and play as if it were the real hole.

LOOK AT THE HOLE ▶

Look at the hole! This tip does not contradict another piece of advice about keeping your head still when you are making the shot. It is a question of watching the hole while you are doing your practice putt to gauge distance. Carry out the same movement when you are making the real shot, taking care to keep your head still.

wrists theory. The first has the advantage of being safer and less random because it is more mechanical.

Fast and slow greens

Before looking at how to tackle these, you need to be aware that a light putter is more suitable for a fast green, and a heavy putter is better for a slow green.

To hit a successful putt on a fast green, your swing should be wide and rhythmic, without any or very little wrist action. The ball is positioned in the center of the stance and the grip can be shortened if necessary for better control. For a compact backswing, put your left hand slightly in front of the ball in the set up position.

If it is a slow green your wrists need to come into operation, and so does your right hand. The ball should be at the extension of your left foot. The grip is at the top of the shaft. Your elbows should be brought in close to your body.

All you have to do now is to hit the ball solidly.

THE CENTURY-OLD LA MOYE GOLF CLUB, ON THE ISLAND OF JERSEY IN THE CHANNEL ISLANDS. IT IS A GOLFER'S PARADISE, WITH ITS PERFECT LINKS, TURF AND FAST GREENS CLOSE TO THE OCEAN.

FOLLOWING PAGES: LA GRANDE MOTTE, ONE OF THE NEW GENERATION OF FRENCH COURSES.

LET THE BALL DROP ▶

To check that your address position is correct, take out another ball and drop it from nose height without modifying your position. In principle, it should fall on top of the one already on the ground or just behind it, but still on the putting line. If it doesn't, your set up position is not right.

REVERSE GRIP

The reverse grip is advised for golfers who cock their wrists and occasionally "yip" the shot. With the reverse grip the left hand is on top of the right and leads. It is easier to keep your right hand pointing toward the hole with this grip.

THE TEXAS WEDGE

This strange term describes the act of "putting from a bunker." It's a good way of salvaging a shot. It is absolutely vital to have an excellent lie in the bunker. Take your stance as for a normal putt. The putter should be slightly above the ball, forcing you to hit lightly as you come down. The grip should be very firm, and you should hit slightly harder than for a normal putt, as you have to hit into the sand and lift the ball up onto the green.

THE HANDS AS AN EXTENSION OF THE CLUB

Cocking your left wrist at impact often causes a putt to go in the wrong direction. To eliminate this error, forget about the ball and concentrate on the top of the club shaft and on both hands, which should be pointing toward the hole.

PLAY BLIND

To help develop feel, practice putting with your eyes closed. Hit three balls, the first one with your eyes open and balls two and three with them shut. The difference is not very great.

ASK FOR THE FLAG

Although you don't need to do this for a short putt, if the distance to be covered is 10 yards (10 m) or more, ask your partner to hold the flag for you. It will help you to judge the distance better. If you practice putting on your carpet at home, position the carpet against a wall, this will act as the flag and you will find that you putt more successfully. Now do the same on the course.

PRACTICE WITH THE TOE ▶

It is tricky to find the ideal place to hit the ball on the putter, in what is called the "sweet spot."

Unfortunately, this often leads to missed putts. To get the right feel, try this easy tip: before playing the course, go to the putting green and try putting with the toe of the putter. This rather strange way of putting will help you to slow down your swing and correct your mistakes.

LISTEN TO THE BALL DROP

If you can manage to hear your ball drop, you will stand a better chance of hitting a good putt. In other words, don't raise your head from the start to the finish of the shot, and lift it only when you hear the characteristic sound of the ball dropping into the hole. This simple method has several advantages, notably that of keeping your head and body still.

PUTTING

◄ PUTTING AROUND THE GREEN

Your ball is less than 2 feet (about 0.5 m) from the edge of the green. You could use your putter. But to prevent the shot from being too hard or too soft, it is wise to hit with the toe of the blade. If you do, the ball will be cushioned, rather than struck. Try it on the putting green and you will be surprised at the results!

THE FLAT PUTTER

One of the reasons for poor putting is that the hands are too close to the body in the set up position. The toe of the putter tends to come up, which often produces a shot to the left or right. When the putter is resting suitably on the ground, there is less risk of a bad trajectory. To rest it on the ground, you will have to move it away from your body slightly when addressing the ball.

ATTACK YOUR PUTTS

An excellent way of attacking your putts is to put a brick behind the hole. You know the old adage, "Never up, never in', in other words, a putt which is not hit confidently, which does not go past the hole, can never go in it. This is why it is very useful to practice 1 or 2 yard (1–2 m) putts using the brick trick. Now pick up the brick and putt to the same place. You will be amazed at your new aggression. This feeling of attacking short putts eliminates any minor borrows or slope on the green which you may not have spotted.

WIDEN YOUR STANCE

Short putts are not always the easiest. Especially those faced under pressure; in such circumstances you need to react by widening your stance in order to stabilize your upper body, lowering the grip so as to play more with your arms and shoulders than with your wrists.

PRACTICE PUTTS AFTER THE BALL ▶

Putts on a slope are never easy to negotiate. This method may help you. Instead of making your practice putt in front of the ball, do it behind the ball. Don't modify your set up position, just extend your arms. Put the putter behind the ball and putt. You will then have a better chance of getting a good line. Now putt for real!

TENNIS TO THE RESCUE ▶

Putting is a question of feel rather than mechanics. To appreciate this, practice for a short time with 5 tennis balls. You have to get them in the hole one after the other. Once you have done this, with some difficulty, putt using golf balls. You will be surprised to find that the hole seems bigger.

GO ALL THE WAY WITH YOUR EYES

Before putting, particularly in the case of sloping putts, it is important to visualize and memorize the trajectory of the shot. Study the line very carefully, you always putt better when you know the contours.

THE COIN

Place a coin in front of the putter and practice putting so that the putter doesn't touch the turf as you hit the ball. If the shot is good, the coin will move slightly.

Short putts

These are supposed to be the easiest, but they are often missed. If you stick to the basic technique, i.e. alignment, body and head still, good pace, there is no reason why you shouldn't hole the putt. Provided the tempo is good, and you don't take too great a backswing, nor accelerate during the backswing or slow down during the downswing. Play short putts straight, without trying to read borrows everywhere. Even if they do exist in reality, they can't have any influence on the trajectory of a firmly struck putt. There is often a tendency to complicate the task instead of simplifying it. There is nothing more frustrating that hitting a short putt which is too short. So aim beyond the hole. If you can do more, you can also do less.

Long putts

To hit a good long putt, you need to pay more attention to the distance than to the direction.

The backswing should be wider, the posture more upright and the grip at the end of the shaft. Try the pendulum method, widen your stance and position the ball at the extension of your left foot.

Uphill putts

This is the easiest putt to negotiate. You need to be aggressive initially, to be successful. If you don't know the green, it is best to attack the putt (place the ball near the left foot to do this), as uphill putts frequently end up too short.

However, there is no need to go from one extreme to the other, as a second downhill putt is not easy to play, as we shall see. It is better to hit a second uphill putt. Pay careful attention to the direction in which the turf lies (i.e. the grain), as this can vary the pace of the shot considerably.

Downhill putts

This is a shot which requires a great deal of feel. After studying the line, and the texture of the turf carefully, do a few practice putts to get an idea of how hard to hit the ball. A downhill putt is particularly tricky because it should scarcely be stroked, and yet should never be short, or you will have another downhill putt to deal with.

How many times have you seen the best players hit a second putt longer than the first! To maximize your chances of success, use the following plan: ball between your feet, open

TWICE U.S. OPEN CHAMPION, CURTIS STRANGE, STUDIES THE LINE OF A PUTT.

PUTTING

BOWLS ▶

Practice by playing bowls. You need at least two people. Two balls each. Aim at a hole, from a fixed point. The hole will be the jack. The first player tries to get near the hole. The second plays one or two balls until he wins the point, i.e. when he places a ball between his opponent's ball and the hole. You never mark it. You never hit the ball more than once. If it goes in the hole, score two points, or else the ball nearest the hole gets one point. This can make putting practice much more interesting than usual.

EXAGGERATE YOUR FOLLOW THROUGH

The reason for putting short is often because the player does not follow-through well with the putter after impact. The ball is yipped and the chances of getting the putt in are virtually non-existent. In practice, don't forget to point the putter at the hole. Exaggerate if necessary to memorize the right sensation.

HEAD OVER THE PUTTER DURING THE FOLLOW THROUGH

To correct too sweeping a backswing and too short a follow-through, reduce your backswing and keep your eyes fixed on the clubhead, making sure that it is directed toward the hole along with the ball. This will help you to keep your head over the ball better.

AIM BEHIND THE HOLE

With short putts, don't just aim at the hole, mark a spot behind the hole and concentrate solely on that.

◄ MAKE THINGS MORE COMPLICATED

Get into the habit of practicing putting by making the hole narrower. To do this, put two tees in front of the hole, thus reducing the access area. When you have to get a real putt in it will all become much easier.

MOVE THE PUTTER AWAY FROM THE BALL

One of the major difficulties with putting is the problem of alignment. To check if your putter is correctly aligned, move it a few inches away from the ball instead of close up to it.

RAILS

It is easier to negotiate a 1 yard (1 m) putt than a 5 yard (5 m) putt. Make yourself some rails on the putting green by placing two tees about two feet from the ball and make yourself putt inside this corridor. Take five or six balls and check out the result. When you are on the course, imagine these markers and look at the hole to judge the distance.

◄ TO ELIMINATE WRIST ACTION

A lot of players tend to use their wrists too much when they are putting. To eliminate this, place the ball further back in relation to your stance. Your hands should be in front of the ball. Your head should be directly over the ball and not behind it.

stance, hands ahead of the putter, square club face. The backswing should be very short, well aligned, and the downswing quicker, with the left hand always "leading." The wrists do not operate. Keep close to the ground in the backswing as well as the downswing to follow the slope. These principles should be memorized and applied.

Raised greens

Very large greens often have two tiers. Everything depends on the difference between the two levels. If your ball is low and the raised area is above it, say about 9 or 10 yards (8 m) away, use the following method: position the ball near the left foot to make it roll, keep a closed stance (right foot behind), elbows in to emphasize the wrist action. During the stroke, the clubhead moves on the inside, and the face opens. It closes as it comes down, and your right hand covers your left hand. You must follow through well and not slice the ball.

Sloping greens

The severely contoured putt is more worthy of special study. So it is important not to waste any

RIGHT:
SEVERIANO BALLESTEROS ALWAYS USES A SUPPLE GRIP WHEN PUTTING.

FACING PAGE:
NANCY LOPEZ PREPARES TO PUTT THROUGH THE SHADOWS. ONE OF THE LEGENDS OF WOMEN'S GOLF, SHE HAS EXCEPTIONAL NATURAL ABILITY AT PUTTING. DO WOMEN HAVE A BETTER TOUCH THAN MEN?

LEFT WRIST STRAIGHT

One of the basic principles of putting is keeping your left wrist straight. To help achieve this, spend a little time on the putting green practicing as follows: secure your left wrist with your right hand. The German golfer Bernhard Langer putts like this.

DISCONNECT YOUR GRIP ▶

Short downhill putts can be real killers. It's difficult to know how to approach them. They are both easy and very difficult. They are easy because they are near the hole, but difficult because they are downhill and the slightest error is exaggerated. It's not unusual to see putts finishing further away from the hole than they were originally. To protect yourself from being over-aggressive, release your grip on the shaft of the club. You will hit the ball less hard, and the shot will be gentler.

PUTT WITH A CHIPPER

Imagine that your ball is just on the edge of the green. You have the choice of using a medium iron – a 5, 6 or 7 – or a putter. A medium iron is advisable in most cases. Play with it as if you were putting. But be careful! The heel of the club should be lifted to insure that the ball doesn't overrun the green. It will enable the ball to get over the edge of the green without rolling too much.

time when you get to the green. Read the slope carefully but quickly, decide upon an intermediate target if the putt is long, look at the direction of the turf and don't hesitate to use the slope if necessary.

The technique to use differs depending on whether the putt has a left to right borrow or one that is right to left. In the first case, the ball must first go to the left, following the slope. It should therefore be positioned near the left foot so that the clubface makes contact as it closes again. The steeper the slope, the further the ball should be aimed to the left. Your stance should be slightly open with the left foot slightly behind. The ball should be struck with the heel of the club in a closed position at impact. The shot should be played with finesse, but not too much. You should still be fairly aggressive. These principles mean nothing without the back-up of practice, which helps generate touch.

When the putt has a right to left borrow, the method is reversed. Only the stance remains open.

In this type of shot, it is quite unusual for the ball to roll a long way because of the slope. Generally, the ball changes its trajectory too soon and goes in front of the hole. It's a shot which

PUTTING CAN BE FRUSTRATING! IN FACT, IT CAN BE THE MOST FRUSTRATING ASPECT OF GOLF. BUT DON'T LET IT GET TO YOU – IT WON'T HELP.

A MIRROR BEHIND THE HOLE

To check if your alignment and aim are good, get a mirror and put it behind the hole. You will be able to see if the blade of the putter is in the right direction.

DRAW A LINE BETWEEN THE BALL AND THE HOLE

A good way of checking the accuracy of a putt is to trace a line between the ball and the hole, so that the ball is positioned in the center of this line. Then position the face of the putter perpendicularly and play with confidence.

TWO PARALLEL CLUBS ▶

If you have difficulty aiming, and this also applies to short putts, put two clubs parallel on each side of the ball, sufficiently far away from the hole and the putter. You will play straight very quickly.

THE FLAG BEHIND THE HOLE

To insure that your ball is not short of the hole, place the flag behind it. Then play as if you were aiming for the flag and not the hole. The exercise consists of getting the ball between the flag and the hole.

THE LADDER SHOT

Put six tees on the green, each one about a yard apart and about 10 yards (10 m) from where you are yourself. The exercise consists of playing the first putt between the first two tees, the second putt between the second and third tees and so on, up to the top of the ladder. You can make it more difficult by trying to touch each tee directly.

TWELVE BALLS AT ONCE

Practice is sometimes tedious. Even the great champions work on their putting by playing fun games. Put three balls at each of the four points on the green representing the cardinal points. Then play them one after the other. You have to keep putting until all twelve balls have been holed consecutively. If one fails to go in, you have to start with the first ball again. The difficulty of this game arises from the distance in relation to the hole. At the start, position yourself at least a yard (1 m) away from the hole, then get further away.

FIVE BALLS ROUND THE HOLE ▶

Place five balls round the hole at an equal distance. Play them one after another. This will develop your sense of direction and will help you to play quickly and decisively.

FORGET ABOUT YOUR HANDS

Hardly any good player uses his hands excessively when putting. The hands are a destabilizing, unbalancing factor, except for long putts. You should try to use only your arms and forearms. Your putting will become more solid and consistent.

MORE PULL

If you pull your putts to the left, a single adjustment may be enough to put it right. Move your left hand to the left on the shaft, and raise the club along the target line, checking that your left hand is pointing toward the hole.

MARKED BALL

To check if you are hitting the ball correctly, mark a new ball with a circle all the way round. If you hit it well, the circled part will be quite visible throughout the shot; if it is not, the contact with the ball was bad.

PUTTING WITH THE DRIVER

No, it's not a joke! To get the right feel when addressing the ball, plus good arm movement and the clubhead on the right trajectory, putt with your driver. The end of the grip is against your stomach. Your hands remain supple and rest freely on the shaft. The position may seem strange but you will soon get used to it.

needs a lot of practice before it is mastered. The same applies to finesse, for unfortunately, no green ever resembles another in golf.

Putting into the wind

If the wind is blowing, you have to adapt. Lean over the ball more to keep your balance, then slightly widen your stance to keep yourself better anchored on the ground, and shorten the shaft. Remember too, that greens are often faster in the wind.

All this is liable to make you lose your rhythm and concentration. It is therefore very important not to panic and to continue to make good contact with the ball, which is not always easy.

Without drawing up an exhaustive list of putting tips, let's look at a few:
– when putting, the arms form a Y with the shoulders, which remain horizontal;
– the thumbs remain on the shaft;
– the head and body stay completely still during the shot;
– you must learn to read the greens in order to assess a potential slope and the speed at which to hit the ball;
– don't be afraid of overrunning the hole. Remember the famous saying, "Never up, never in."

In a chapter on Putting, we could talk at length about the curious phenomenon of "yips," an affliction which affects a number of players at all levels, and which is very hard to eliminate. It is basically a problem of confidence. If you are unfortunate enough to fall victim to it, the best way of curing it is to go back to the basics or to change your way of putting radically. Or change your putter.

THE PLUMBLINE METHOD OF READING A GREEN. IT IS USED MORE FREQUENTLY THAN PEOPLE REALIZE, EVEN THOUGH ITS POPULARITY HAS TENDED TO DECREASE.

WEIGHT ON THE HEELS

Keeping your head still is essential in putting, particularly with short putts. If you turn your head, you have little chance of getting the putt in the hole.

A good way of keeping your head still is to stand in the set up position on your heels, and stay like it throughout the shot.

It is in fact very difficult to keep your balance on your heels if your head moves. Try it and you will see.

DISTANCE IN LONG PUTTS

With all long putts you will be told – and it is right – that distance is the most important thing. Ultimately it doesn't matter whether you are a yard (1 m) to the right or left. That is better than a putt which is too short or which overruns the hole by 5 yards (5 m).

TEES ON THE GREEN

You have to know how to judge the distance of the ball from the hole and play confidently when you are putting. One good exercise consists of pushing in some tees at different points on the green and putting to them successively from different angles.

IF THE BALL JUMPS UP

Sometimes if you try too hard to keep close to the ground during the backswing, the ball jumps up at the start of the shot. To avoid this and to give the ball a straighter line, try to hit it in the middle rather than at the bottom. Don't be afraid to lift the club gently during the backswing. The ball will go better.

DON'T MOVE AT THE TOP OF THE BACKSWING

If you are playing in a strong wind, you will soon realize how hard it is to putt well under these conditions. If you tend to lose your normal rhythm, practice holding the putter at the top of the backswing for a few seconds before coming down. Repeat this several times, reducing the length of time at the top of the backswing each time you try it.

PRACTICE

Can someone become a great pianist without devoting several hours a day to practicing? Of course not. The same applies to golf. It's not a question of turning you into a champion – you couldn't learn that from a book anyway. More simply put, to become a good weekend player, you don't need to have great talents, just some experience of playing, backed up by sufficient practice to enable you to cope with any situation which may arise.

I think golf can be considered in various ways. Clearly the player who wants to turn professional and make their career in the game must make themselves practice regularly. On the other hand if the aim is to have a handicap of 18, this can be achieved quickly by using the correct techniques. If you play other ball games it is an advantage. A keen tennis or hockey player will be able to hit the ball well more quickly and will soon acquire the right feel. This doesn't in any way absolve a player from practicing at least once a week, particularly at the beginning.

What is the best way to use your practice time? First of all, by having a clear idea of what you want to do. You often hear the following remark: "Practicing is boring." My response is that it depends entirely on you. There are a hundred and one ways to make practice more enjoyable. All the tips in this book are intended precisely to make golf more enjoyable. But you also need to

HOWEVER TEDIOUS IT
MAY SEEM, PRACTICE IS A
VITAL PREREQUISITE FOR
IMPROVING YOUR GAME.
IT IS ESPECIALLY
IMPORTANT FOR
BEGINNERS.

stick to certain rules if your practicing is to be effective. You need to know what shot you should play before you hit the ball.

Next, try to follow the basic fundamentals of the swing; concentrate on your weaknesses. These may consist of an alignment error, the wrong grip, poor rhythm, a bad swing plane. Work on your good points too.

Work in stages

Don't start your practice session with a driver, which is the most difficult club to use. Hit the first five balls as slowly as possible. It doesn't matter where they go. Then get out a wedge, and gradually go up the clubs, spending a little more time on the 7 iron. Don't hit more than ten balls per club. Hit an extra five balls with the driver, in addition to practicing a specific point. If you have serious problems with your swing, go back to the 7 iron and give it the time it needs. Hit slowly, like all good players. Practice doesn't consist of spraying balls around as if you were using a machine gun! Hitting softly lets your muscles warm up gradually, but it also removes any concern over accuracy.

PROGRESS

When you are practicing, you need to think about good rhythm in particular. Don't try to hit the ball too fast. To achieve this rhythm, alternate your clubs, starting with a 9 iron. Then go on to a 5 iron, then an 8, then a 4, finishing up with a 7 followed by a 3. Try to get the same feel with each club, whether it is a short or long iron.

THE IMPORTANCE OF THE HANDS

Although the hands shouldn't be excessively important, they need to be strong. To develop this strength, the famous Henry Cotton recommended repeatedly hitting at an old tire. Its resistance is a sure way of testing your resistance. Practice this exercise little and often.

A similar type of exercise is to swing with one hand against the tire, preferably the stronger one. You will also notice that this highlights a poor grip.

DAILY ROUTINE

The most difficult thing is to plan a daily training session before you go to work.

Here's an example, which lasts about thirty minutes.
1. Warm up with a heavier club than the one you would normally use. Do some preliminary gentle practice swings, increasing the tempo little by little, then some complete practice swings.
2. Stand in front of a mirror and dissect your swing. Hold each stage of the swing for ten seconds and then go on to the next.
3. To toughen up your hands, hit against an old tire for about ten minutes.
4. Do some swings at shoulder height and some horizontally with a sand wedge.
5. Do a few practice swings with different clubs.

PRETEND

If you haven't the time to hit practice balls, just do this: practice shadowing swings as if you were playing a real ball, and following the basic principles of the swing. You will be warmed up and ready to start your game very quickly.

TWO CLUBS

If you haven't time to hit balls before playing, take two clubs out of your bag and have a quick practice swing using both together. It is hard to manipulate them at first, but when you go back to playing with just one club, it feels as if you only have a pen in your hand. It will help the whole swing.

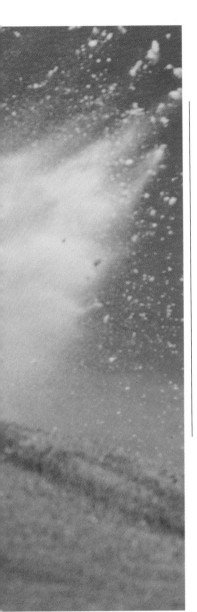

One of the purposes of practice is to eliminate weaknesses in your game. To do this, you need to imagine you are in an actual game situation. Act as if you were on the course and invent a scenario which creates a variety of shots to be played. It has been proved that a scorecard is often ruined simply because a player doesn't know how to deal with specific difficulties. Hazards like bunkers are too often neglected. A golf course includes an average of about sixty bunkers. It would be presumptuous to think that your ball will avoid them all! Because of their placement, they tend most often to attract balls hit by average rather than good or indeed great players. Here, as elsewhere, prevention is better than cure, and it is best not to feel despondent every time your ball finds the sand. The only way to avoid this is to work on this kind of shot in practice. But

unfortunately practice is often a secondary consideration.

Final tips for success

Split up your practice session, take a few breaks, discuss something with a friend. Try to practice on turf rather than on carpet if possible. It is always better to recreate actual game situations. Before you play, decide whether you are going to work on a particular shot, or whether you are going to master the club you're holding in your hand. The former is best.

Bearing all this advice in mind, be confident and remember, golf is 10 percent talent and 90 percent sweat, as Picasso said about something quite different.

AMERICAN RYDER CUP
GOLFER CHIP BECK IS A
MASTER OF THE SHORT
GAME.

SWING THE SHAFT ▶

To get the feel of a good follow-through, practice swinging the shaft of the club. This may seem strange at first, but you will soon realize that you can speed up the club. When you are practicing, get into the habit of alternating a real shot with swinging the grip of the club.

BE IMAGINATIVE

Use your imagination to vary your practice sessions. Choose a few specific points to work on, recreate hazards, a fairway, the rough, etc.

WORK ON THE IMPORTANT SHOTS

Statistics show that the short game and putting form well over half the game. Only 25 percent of the time is devoted to using woods and 14 percent to using irons, 5 percent is spent on recovery shots, 13 percent on chipping and .... 43 percent on putting! So it's pretty vital to work on that short game.

PLAY WITH A HEADCOVER

To check if your swing plane is correct, lay the headcover of your driver 2 inches (5 cm) to the side of the ball, parallel with the target. If you don't touch the cover when you are playing, then your club has a good inside-to-inside swing trajectory.

HAVE A BREAK

It is not always a good thing to play too much. There is such a thing as being "over-golfed." It is also important to relax and not to set yourself impossible targets. For good motivation, take a break. A few days ski-ing in the winter will do you a lot of good! When you go back to playing again, your desire to achieve great things will be greatly increased and your motivation will be strengthened.

STRATEGY

A golfer cannot simultaneously have the desire to make progress and look on golf as a mere pastime, as an unimportant but pleasant leisure activity. The two attitudes are blatantly contradictory. In other words, golf is a serious game, and it deserves to be approached as such. Strategy is one of the areas which calls upon a player's intelligence. While 50 percent of success is represented by technique, the other 50 percent is mental. Golf is different from other more "mechanical" sports in this respect.

It is often said that "Golf is played inside the head." That's true, but golf is also played by using your head. It is interesting to observe just how different golfers seem when they are playing at their own club, and when they go elsewhere. At home, they have familiar markers, they recognize every inch of turf, and, in short, they achieve flattering scores. It is often very different when they are confronted with a situation for which they are unprepared. Concepts of distance, speed of greens, and wind all differ. The concept of strategy and a knowledge of the game play a vital role at times like this.

One of the great advantages of golf is that it is played on very different terrains, in very different surroundings. A Scottish links course has very little in common with a golf course on the outskirts of Phoenix. A course in the mountains is nothing like one on the plain. You have to adapt

GOLF IS ALSO A GAME WHICH INVOLVES REFLECTION. BIG HITTERS ARE NOT ALWAYS THE BEST PLAYERS. YOU NEED TO KNOW HOW TO CALCULATE, NEGOTIATE, AND ADAPT TO MULTIPLE SITUATIONS. THE GOOD PLAYER FINDS THE APPROPRIATE SOLUTION FOR EVERY KIND OF SHOT.

LEFT:
CHOOSING THE RIGHT CLUB IS VITAL TO THE SUCCESS OF A SHOT. THERE IS AN AVERAGE DIFFERENCE OF TWO CLUBS BETWEEN THE COMPETENT GOLFER AND A PLAYER LIKE GREG NORMAN. DON'T PRETEND YOU ARE A CHAMPION. CHOOSING A LONGER CLUB ALLOWS YOU TO PLAY A MORE RELAXED SHOT.

FACING PAGE:
THE BRITISH PLAYER NICK FALDO IS CONSIDERED TO BE ONE OF THE BEST STRATEGISTS IN THE WORLD. HIS VICTORY IN THE 1987 BRITISH OPEN AT MUIRFIELD, WHEN HE SCORED PARS ON EVERY HOLE IN THE FINAL ROUND, CEMENTED THIS REPUTATION.

in a lasting way. Every average or low handicap player should always bear in mind the following essential rule: you never hit the same shot twice in golf. So you musn't hit all your shots in the same way. A good lie is less frequent on the course itself than on the practice area; your feet are not always flat on the ground and the route to the hole is strewn with hazards. You need to take time to think, as each shot is an isolated shot, and should be thought of as such. This is one of the great difficulties of the game.

If you follow the advice below, you will soon lower your score by several strokes.

Be positive

This may seem a statement of the obvious, yet many players seem to view golf as a punishment, and do not feel happy out on the course. You need to be humble in golf. If you cannot accept that you will hit bad shots, it's not worth carrying on. It is a well-known fact that you will hit more bad shots than good ones. On the other hand, a positive attitude implies knowing how to "play badly well," i.e. in terms of your scorecard it is better to hit four average shots than three good shots and one bad one.

PRACTICING AT YOUR HOME CLUB

If you are a member of a club, or are used to playing a particular course, there will probably be two or three holes which you find especially hard to tackle successfully. The best way to "exorcise" this feeling might be to put it down on paper. Sketch the holes which make you suffer, and look at reasonable solutions for solving your problems. Next time you play it is quite likely that you will be less daunted by these holes as you will have thought about how best to deal with them.

WORK ON YOUR STRONG POINTS

When you are practicing, it is important to work on your strong points to develop confidence. Play your wood or favorite iron and content yourself with holing 1 yard (1 m) putts on the putting green.

PLAY YOUR OWN GAME

One of the most difficult aspects of golf is playing your natural game. Play the shots and select the clubs that suit you best; choose a tactic that comes naturally to you and don't be influenced by your opponent.

TO REGAIN YOUR FEEL

In golf, as in most other things, it is often necessary to move from the most difficult thing to the easiest. For example, if you feel you are not making contact with the ball as well as you do normally, don't hesitate to go and hit a few shots from a fairly shallow bunker. Contact with the ball in this situation has to be perfect, or the ball won't move. You should use a compact swing and don't dig your feet into the sand too deeply. When you are back on a flat, hard surface, everything will seem much easier.

PUTTING ON CARPET

This is an easy exercise to practice in your living-room. Putt against the skirting board along a wall of the room. This will help you to putt consistently every time. But be careful, it is important to lift the club slightly on the inside during the backswing!

APPROACH TO THE GREEN

It is a common belief that you should use a more lofted club the nearer you are to the green. For example, a sand wedge on the edge of the green. Wrong. If there is no hazard between you and the flag, it is advisable to hit a rolled approach shot using a 7 or 8 iron. If the ground is rough, or you have to get past a hazard, then it is better to use a 9 iron or a pitching wedge to make a lifted approach shot.

DON'T ADD UP YOUR SCORE UNTIL THE END

Everyone should know that the game isn't over until the last putt. How many times have good players, even champions, lost everything at the final hole, simply because they are too concerned that they must achieve a certain score. The best approach is to give each hole everything you've got, and not add up your total score until all eighteen holes have been played. If this is too hard, wait until you have played the first nine holes to add up your first half, then carry on to the 18th.

LIVE FOR THE MOMENT

Golf is a sport that requires much thought in between shots. So it is important to concentrate at the right moments, and not constantly over a four-hour period, which would be ridiculous. When you approach the ball, you should be capable of thinking only of the shot you are going to play, without losing confidence, and relaxing completely between shots.

CONCENTRATE

"Concentration" is definitely one of the words which is least understood by golfers. "Concentration" does not mean "tensing up," but the opposite. Before tackling a shot, you need to be able to visualize the end result. The great golfer should have a good swing, but above all he must be able to analyze the situation perfectly in his head.

RELY ON THE OUT OF BOUNDS

On some holes beginners, and even more experienced players, get worried about driving when there is an out-of-bounds area beside the hole. Often they avoid it by inserting their tee on the side furthest away from this part of the course. This reaction is understandable but must be avoided. Let's take the example of a par 4 with a dog-leg to the left. The ideal drive would be to position the ball at the corner of the dog-leg on the right side of the fairway, with the out-of-bounds area or hazard such as a wood situated on the left of the hole. You need to line up with the tee as near as possible to the out-of-bounds area. You will then have lots of space to drive to the right of the fairway. You get a better view of the hole and avoid the danger, in this case on the left, more easily. Good players may even hit a draw from right to left, taking advantage of the right side of the fairway after teeing off from the left of the teeing area.

Conclusion: out-of-bounds area to the left, drive from the left; out-of-bounds area to the right, drive from the right.

PLANE? WHAT PLANE? GOLFING HAZARDS CAN APPEAR IN ALL SHAPES AND SIZES. AUSTRALIAN GOLFER PETER SENIOR SEEMS UNPERTURBED HOWEVER BY THIS LOW-FLYING AIRCRAFT DURING THE 1992 AUSTRALIAN OPEN.

152

STRATEGY

PLAY YOUR BEST SHOT

You get good days and bad days in golf, like anything else. You need to appreciate this. Don't imagine that hitting a little white ball is inevitably peaceful! This is one of the reasons why you need to know how to cash in on your strengths when things are not going as well as you would like. For example, on a long par 3 hole, liberally sprinkled with bunkers, it is often better to play safe with a 3 wood than to tempt providence with a 3 iron hit hard. If you are unsure of your club, use the one you feel most confident with.

VISUALIZE THE SHOT TO PLAY

If you watch the great players, you will notice that preparation is vital, and that it is always done in the same way. Jack Nicklaus is the best example of a golfer who always considers his shot carefully before playing it. They never get their club out of the bag before they have visualized the shape and trajectory of their intended shot. It is important to imagine yourself playing the shot.

SET A TARGET

You have a par 5 hole with a very wide fairway, and you don't know where to hit the ball. Why not aim at a target, perhaps a tree or something else which will help you to align yourself better and hit a more accurate drive?

PLAY TO YOUR STRENGTHS

Instead of playing all sorts of shots, play only to your strengths, and use the same type of shot whenever you can.

For example, if you know how to play a fade (left to right spin), try to perfect the shot and match the course to your game.

PLAY YOUR 3 WOOD

If you are driving poorly, but are afraid of losing distance with your tee shot by using a long iron instead of a driver, still use a driver, but lower your grip. This enables you to control the club more easily and gives better body balance and a position closer to the ball. If you prefer to play safe, use your 3 wood. The difference is not that great, and you will hit the ball with a lower trajectory by using a more aggressive swing.

PLAY A 1 IRON IF YOU CAN

This tip is only for experienced players. Using a 1 or 2 iron is not the easiest thing to do. But this kind of club has a dual advantage. It has greater accuracy in comparison with the driver, and it avoids hazards which, as we all know, are positioned within the range of the driver. It is better to hit a slightly shorter shot into the middle of the fairway than a 250 yard (250 m) drive into the wood.

After all, there is scarcely any difference in difficulty between playing a 6 iron or an 8 iron for your approach to the green.

LEARN HOW TO CONFRONT THE SLOW PLAYER

Slow play is the bane of modern golf. It is creeping in more and more and is very difficult to curb. If you find yourself in this situation, and you will, sooner or later, do not let it spoil your game. You must tell yourself that you can't do anything about it, and instead of getting annoyed with your opponent, remain calm and concentrate on your own game. If the situation really becomes intolerable, drop in a few remarks like "If this goes on, I'll have to call the referee" (only valid for competitions) or,

instead of chatting to your opponent, head off briskly toward your ball after playing your drive. Your opponent will get the message.

WHISTLE WHILE YOU PLAY

Sing, whistle, relax between shots. There is no better way of preparing for the next shot. It may seem silly but it's very effective. It also helps you forget about bad shots.

GET RID OF USELESS CLUBS ▶

Use the rule of a maximum of fourteen clubs in your bag to your advantage. If you are playing in a competition, are you sure that all your long irons are indispensable? Why don't you take another putter or even a third wedge in addition to your sand wedge and pitching wedge? Third solution: carry a 5 or 7 wood instead of a long iron. Next, when you are playing a friendly game, get used to playing with a half-set. You will be amazed at the results. Often the difference in score is minimal.

WATCH THE BALL

You are standing on the 18th tee and in a fine position to get a really good score. On this long par 4 hole, your ball goes into the rough. Disgusted, you turn away and lose any chance you may have had of finding it. Many players adopt this negative attitude! On the contrary, you should be positive. Watch the ball and use a marker in your attempt to find it. Before leaving the tee, play a provisional ball and tell your opponent what you are doing. This will mean that you don't have to return to the tee if you can't find your ball.

STRATEGY

◀ LEAVES IN THE AIR

The flag is not always the best indicator of wind direction, particularly from a distance. In addition, the green might be sheltered by trees and give a false impression of calm. The best method of gauging the wind is to throw a handful of grass or leaves into the air and see how they fall. You could also look at the treetops, which will tell you the wind direction much more accurately.

BECOME LEFT-HANDED

We know that the left side is very important in golf. Natural right-handers often neglect this aspect. To absorb this idea better, some coaches advise that you learn to play shots left-handed. It requires a lot of practice – you can't become left-handed overnight.

PLAY TO THE BACK OF THE GREEN

If you analyze your game you will notice that your most common mistakes in terms of club selection involve using clubs which are too short. This applies to approach shots in particular, where the ball often finishes at the front of the green rather than near the flag. Why? Because players tend to aim at the flag rather than the back of the green, allowing themselves some margin for error. Don't be afraid to play long; more often than not you will find the ball ends up nearer to the hole.

THINK POSITIVE IN THE ▶ WOOD

If your ball is unlucky enough to land among some trees, analyze the situation clearly. Without trying to be a Ballesteros, study all the possibilities. Whether the opening is too small and there is nothing for it but to take a penalty, or whether there is a small but real chance of success which should be taken. Use as much space as is physically available and play confidently, especially if the lie is good and your swing is not restricted by the branches of a tree, for example. Next, decide on the

Being positive includes knowing that if you have a 24 handicap, you are entitled to "commit" twelve bogeys and six double bogeys. This leaves a good margin for error, and if you bear it in mind, you have a good chance of playing to a standard (and score) that is better than your handicap.

Be methodical

Always prepare for a shot in the same way. Point the club face toward the target, take up your stance, look at the target again, do a few practice swings, (waggle!) and visualize the shot. "Go to the movies," as Jack Nicklaus would say.

Be patient

Once again our model is Jack Nicklaus. You should never force things. If you think that you must par a certain hole to win the monthly medal, you are putting unnecessary pressure on yourself. Since golf is a game of nerves, there is no point in putting them on edge. It is better to stay relaxed under all circumstances, even after a birdie and especially after a bogey!

THE GOLF COURSE AT BOSSEY ON THE FRENCH-SWISS BORDER. ONE OF THE TOUGHEST AND MOST DRAMATIC COURSES IN EUROPE.

exact place that the ball should land, just as you would for a normal shot.

HAVE YOUR OWN PAR

A double or triple bogey is often explained by a player being a little too greedy. If you have a long par 4 ahead of you, and you're not a long hitter, try thinking: "From my point of view, this is more like a par 5, so I'm going to try to get onto the green in three shots, plus two putts, making 5."

CONCENTRATE ON A PARTICULAR POINT

If you are having adjustment problems, ask yourself: "What's wrong?" and try to solve the problem step by step. It's not helpful to clutter your mind with lots of different theories. It's better to think of one thing at a time.

Be clear

Accept your limitations. Don't over-extend yourself just to try and match the "big boys."

For example, you often see players trying to hit very hard with a 9 iron when a comfortable 8 or 7 iron would do the job perfectly well. There is about 10 yards (10 m) difference between two clubs. On a green measuring 30 yards (30 m) long, there might be two or three clubs difference.

One good strategy might also be to take a 3 wood instead of a driver when the fairway is narrow, and use a long iron rather than a 3 wood on a par 5 where there is no real prospect of reaching the green in two shots. Try not to cut the corner of a dogleg, however tempting, use a wedge instead of a 6 or 7 iron in the rough etc. Aggression does not always pay in golf. A hundred and one different things can make the difference between a good and a bad score card.

Some strategy errors

– Failing to warm up before a game and failing to reach the 1st tee until the last minute;

– Hitting your practice shots too quickly, just to make up for lost time;

– Playing from the wrong side of the tee;

– Bad alignment: if you set up poorly without thinking, you will have to compensate somehow;

– Using the wrong club, especially in the wind;

– Attempting miraculous recovery shots when common sense should prevail. Not everyone's name is Ballesteros.

– Choosing the wrong club, particularly in the short game: a wedge instead of a rolled 7 or 8 iron;

– Teeing off badly: with the driver, the top of the clubhead should not be above the middle of the ball; with a 3 wood, the top of the club should be at two thirds the height of the ball.

157

THREE RULES OF THE GAME TO OBSERVE

You should not clutter your head with endless theories which will only complicate things, instead of simplifying them. Stick to three basic rules: keep as far away from hazards as possible; on a dogleg, aim at the widest part of the fairway; choose the largest area of the green, especially if the flag is next to a bunker. Bear these simple rules in mind when you are playing your round.

KEEP YOUR COOL

It is vital to keep your head when you are playing golf. Particularly when things are going badly, but also when they are going well, for it is then that the adrenalin level rises quickly and rhythm can be lost. If you have ever made consecutive birdies, you will know what I mean! You need to slow down the "machine." Take your time, slow down your tempo, your walking speed, think carefully but not excessively, as hesitation is not helpful.

THINK ABOUT YOUR GOOD SHOTS

When you look at your scorecard you will often discover that there have been just two or three bad holes, often one after another, that have ruined your score. Instead of dwelling on the bad points, which are inevitable anyway, adopt a positive attitude and remember the good shots. During a round of golf, have fun counting only your good shots rather than the score. After a while, when you start to play a "normal" game, your score will probably be better.

THE ARMCHAIR SHOT

Usually after a round of golf, you forget everything until the next game. That's fine, as it helps to eliminate problems, but if you have played well, take five minutes to contemplate why you did so well.

NEVER APOLOGIZE

When you are playing with a friend, the most important thing is to play to the best of your ability, without ever saying "Sorry" for a bad shot. Everyone hits bad shots, and that is not what counts. The important thing is to complement each other and play with confidence.

GOLF FOR WOMEN, JUNIORS, AND SENIORS

Women's golf

Are men and women so different that it is necessary for a different golf swing to be taught to each sex?

In the main, the answer is "No." The golf swing stays basically the same, with a few adaptations. These are based on facts which show that women golfers tend to struggle with identical and easily identifiable problems.

There are often problems with posture, with the wrist in the backswing, with overswinging, lack of rotation, a bent left arm or lack of leg action during the downswing. In virtually every case, the cure is the same as the one described in the preceding chapters. Women often cock their left wrist at the top of the backswing due to having too tight a grip in the set up. Many women golfers overswing and lift their hands too high to compensate for inadequate rotation. Result: the upper body moves first in the downswing, the club advances too rapidly and the right shoulder is too

FORMER FRENCH CHAMPION, MARIE-LAURE DE LORENZI, EUROPEAN NUMBER ONE IN 1988 AND 1989.

active and goes over the top.

Generally, women who do not have the necessary physique needed to hit the ball a long way should compensate by trying to generate as much clubhead speed as possible.

To hit as far as possible, a woman needs a very wide swing arc so that the clubhead travels the greatest distance before impact, but this can give rise to problems of overswinging.

Nevertheless, the risk must be taken. Because women are naturally more supple than men, they must take advantage of their attributes. There still remains the problem of controlling the clubhead and of eliminating unnecessary body movement during the downswing.

On the course itself, women are very capable of analyzing the different situations which arise. They are often more sensible or rational than men, and choose the more reasonable option, enabling them to reach the green without too many potential pitfalls.

It is a fact that everything is won or lost on the fairway for the average woman golfer. She needs to program each of her shots, recognize her limitations and the distances for each club, and draw her own conclusions.

Once on the green, women often have a better touch than men, and often need only the minimum number of putts. If a woman player putts with confidence, she can be aggressive and a formidable opponent. "Tell me how you putt and I'll tell you who you are," – a phrase particularly true in the case of women.

Because women tend to be well-organized, plan ahead, and have an excellent analytical sense and good touch, they are generally very impressive on and around the green. They never think they are beaten, and are feared adversaries, perhaps because they consider golf as a discipline as well as a game. Frequent practice allows good feel to become ingrained, and women tend to gain experience and maturity more quickly than men players.

Junior golf

Before talking about technical things, I feel it is important to caution those parents who, frustrated because they have never played themselves, transfer all their ambitions onto their offspring. This often happens without any consideration of the fact that a child is very vulnerable at fourteen or fifteen, and has not yet settled upon the pursuit of any activity in particular. If you impose a sport

IT IS NOT A GOOD IDEA TO
START GOLF TOO YOUNG;
10-12 IS A GOOD AGE.
JACK NICKLAUS STARTED
PLAYING WHEN HE WAS
10 AND GREG NORMAN
BEGAN AT 15.

like golf on such a child when he or she has no desire to practice, it may have the effect of putting them off the game irrevocably. The best solution seems to me to give a child complete freedom to maneuver and introduce him or her to as many different sports as possible, so building good coordination and the necessary reflexes.

What Age Should They Start?
You can begin to get your child interested in golf at the age of eleven or twelve by teaching him or her the basics as well as the right principles, the "fundamentals," as they are called – without applying any pressure at all. On the other hand, it is important for a child to have an idea of the golf swing at a fairly early stage. Natural suppleness will make the action more natural and it will stick, regardless of what happens. Golf is too technical a sport to begin at thirty years of age.

Golf courses are not usually designed with children in mind, and young people often get very frustrated at not being able to hit a par 4 in two shots or a par 5 in three, in spite of an apparently fluid, effective swing. It is obvious that a thirteen-year-old child, unless unusually gifted, is going to be less powerful than an adult. However, he will have other physical qualities apart from strength which can compensate. For example, normally children have enough energy to impart good clubhead acceleration at impact.

The most important thing at this age is to understand the basics, and to work on "grooving" the swing, so that it becomes automatic. Even if practice is not always fun, children should not start to play on the course itself too soon. A bad score can be very discouraging, and we all know how important results are to a child. They need to be competitive but also to enjoy golf for its own sake.

Lastly, teach them at an early stage about golf course etiquette, to have respect for it and to be honest with themselves.

When starting to play, children should have a 5 iron, a 7 iron and a putter in their bags. Later they can add a 3 wood, a 3 and 9 iron and a wedge. This will teach them how to use the different clubs.

Children don't need lessons every week to improve. Being very observant, they will make a lot of progress by watching the best players at the club or by watching a tournament. Their ability to mimic may surprise you. It is by developing a lack of self-consciousness which gives the best results.

A child has all the qualities needed to succeed at golf except perhaps one: patience! It is hard to ask a child to concentrate for four hours, and expect them to think about which shot to play next. On the other hand, a relaxed approach to the game, a generally positive attitude, instinct and straightforward technique are all plus points which many adults envy. We should think more of golf as something to be enjoyed; so many players don't look as if they are having much fun when they are on the course. We are too busy thinking about the swing we have just made. This is another area in which adults differ from children.

Senior golf

There are two types of senior golfer. The first type is the player who has played for years and only needs to make a few minor adjustments to continue to enjoy the game. The second type of player, i.e. the "beginner senior" has more need of advice because it is hard to take up a new sport after the age of fifty, especially when it involves a swing or a body movement which is highly technical and does not come naturally.

Unlike many other sports, senior golf does not consist of disadvantages alone. The best proof of this lies in the success of the U.S. Senior Tour,

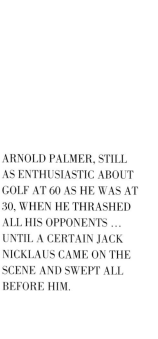

ARNOLD PALMER, STILL
AS ENTHUSIASTIC ABOUT
GOLF AT 60 AS HE WAS AT
30, WHEN HE THRASHED
ALL HIS OPPONENTS …
UNTIL A CERTAIN JACK
NICKLAUS CAME ON THE
SCENE AND SWEPT ALL
BEFORE HIM.

where "former champions" are still scoring regularly in the 60s. Age brings experience and maturity, which counteract any loss on the physical side. Of course, there are relatively few examples of golfers who play better at fifty than at thirty, but it is not unrealistic to hope to do well at a late stage in one's career. You need to practice seriously, live a healthy life-style and be motivated. The degree of enthusiasm among golfers over fifty can be quite amazing. After years and years of frustration at not being able to play regularly, they can now give free rein to their pursuits. They enjoy practicing. They achieve surprising scores, without getting too over-excited! Their swing may have deteriorated slightly, but they have compensated for it with a more effective short game. In short, they know how to adapt their technique.

They use their putter to play from the edge of the green, and even from the bunker, learning to play a lobbed ball and chipping with a 7 iron. All these skills can be acquired and practiced. When there is more time to devote to your passion, and when you have less stamina, the short game is the best way of maintaining a good handicap. It is pointless trying to hit the ball as far as you did twenty years ago.

THE 16TH HOLE ON THE FAMOUS VINTAGE COURSE IN THE MIDDLE OF THE CALIFORNIAN DESERT. A TOTALLY ARTIFICIAL ENVIRONMENT CREATED OUT OF A WILD AND HOSTILE NATURAL SETTING.

The swing should evolve after fifty. The accent should be more on hand and arm action. You should think of a lighter material for your clubs, perhaps graphite. You will need to make a few adjustments to help turn your shoulders: have a narrower, more open stance when addressing the ball, lifting the left heel during the backswing. Use fairway woods to get out of the rough, such as the 7 wood, which, because of its design, allows you to escape from the most difficult situations.

Even if your long game has not deteriorated significantly, putting will become a problem. The explanation may be simple. It could be a question of eyesight, or a lack of feeling in the hands. It is always the case that putting becomes harder with age. The mere fact of not being able to putt as aggressively as before can induce doubt and uncertainty.

If a golfer suffers from arthritis, as happened to the great American champion Gene Sarazen, who couldn't play without plunging his hands into a bucket of hot water beforehand, or if he has a bad back, then it becomes a more restricting activity. Especially when you have played for a number of years. Golfers who start to play after the age of fifty very soon wish they had started earlier. They really get stuck in, however, and whether they are talented, or simply hard workers, they will have lots of pleasure to look forward to – which, after all, is what counts in the long run! The pleasure of the game should prevail. Senior golfers can often teach us a salutary lesson.

GLOSSARY

ADDRESS: player's position in front of the ball before playing.

ALBATROSS: achieving a score of 3 under par on one hole (2 on a par 5 or 1 on a par 4).

APPROACH SHOT: shot intended to reach a nearby green.

BACKSPIN: backward spin on the ball. A ball with a lot of backspin will not roll very far along the ground after it has landed.

BACKSWING: describes the lifting of the club, the first moving part of the action of actually hitting the ball.

BIRDIE: score of 1 under par on a hole, for example a 3 on a par 4 hole.

BOGEY: score of 1 over par on a hole, for example, a 5 on a par 4 hole.

BUNKER: a hollow filled with sand, sometimes cavernous in nature. Its purpose is to make the course more difficult and penalize bad strokes.

CADDIE: carries a golfer's clubs and accompanies the player round the course.

CHIP SHOT: approach shot intended to position the ball near the hole.

CLEAN: shot where the player makes direct contact with the ball.

CLUB: golf implement used to propel the ball by hitting it.

DIVOT: clump of turf which the golfer dislodges with his club when playing; the player should replace the turf so as not to damage the course.

DOGLEG: a hole curving sharply to the left (left dogleg) or to the right (right dogleg).

DOWNSWING: describes the descent of the club, the second part of the swing which brings the club into contact with the ball.

DRIVER: name commonly given to the number 1 wood.

DROPPING: action of picking up a ball which is in an unplayable position and putting it back into play by dropping it (often under penalty) in front of oneself, with the arm extended at shoulder height.

EAGLE: score of 2 under par on a hole, for example a 2 on a par 4 hole.

ETIQUETTE: set of principles defining the attitude and behavior a player should adopt in respect of the course itself and toward other players.

EXPLOSION: approach shot out of a bunker. The ball is not hit directly, but the player hits the sand just before it.

FADE: trajectory of a ball which curves slightly to the right at the end of its flight.

FAIRWAY: part of the course where the grass is cut fairly short, between the tee area and the green.

FLUFFING: a missed shot, where the ground is hit before the ball.

GREEN: part of the course surrounding the hole, where the grass is cut very short and rolled as smooth as possible.

GRIP: method of holding the shaft of the club with the hands. Also, part of the shaft where the hands are placed.

HANDICAP: method of classification for amateur golfers.

HOOK: flight of a ball veering to the right before coming back in sharply from the left.

IMPACT: exact moment when the club strikes the ball.

INLAND: a course built inland, away from the coast.

IRON: club whose narrow head is made of metal. Irons are numbered from 1 to 9. The pitching wedge and the sand wedge are also made of iron.

LIE: angle formed by the shaft of the club and the ground; also, the position of the ball on the turf.

LINKS: a course constructed near the sea; most links courses are in Great Britain and Ireland.

LOFT: angle of openness of the clubface in relation to the shaft.

MATCH PLAY: method of playing when two players oppose each other directly and score against each other, as against the course.

MEDAL PLAY OR STROKE PLAY: method of playing in which all the strokes played by a golfer over eighteen holes are added up.

NIBLICK: ancient club corresponding to a modern 9 iron.

OPEN: competition open to professionals and amateurs of any nationality.

PAR: reference score for a hole. The holes are par 3, 4 or 5, calculated according to the length of the hole.

PITCH: approach shot intended to lift the ball high in the air; also a small hole in the grass made by the ball when it falls on the green or fairway.

PITCHING WEDGE: a fairly heavy club with a very open face. Used a lot for approach shots.

PLAY-OFF: final part of a competition, in which the eventual winner is discovered after the playing of an extra hole or holes.

PLUGGED: description of a ball dug in or buried in the rough, fairway or sand.

POSTURE: position of the body at address.

PRACTICE GROUND: area usually close to the clubhouse where the players practice their strokes. Coaches and professionals give lessons here.

PULL: a ball shooting off to the left in a straight line.

PUSH: a ball shooting off to the right in a straight line.

PUTTER: club with a vertical face, for use on the green.

PUTTING: part of the game consisting of making the ball roll across the green toward the hole.

RECOVERY: a shot saved, generally out of the rough or from a particular hazard.

ROLLED SHOT: approach shot played very close to the green. The ball stays low but rolls a lot.

ROUGH: part of the course which borders the fairway on each side, situated close to the green. It is sometimes very difficult to get the ball out on to the fairway or green.

SAND WEDGE: heaviest club in the bag, with the most open face. Used a lot in bunkers close to the green, when using the explosion technique.

SET: group of up to fourteen clubs available to the golfer.

SLICE: the trajectory of a ball going to the left before curving round to the right;

SHANKING OR SOCKETING: a completely uncontrolled shot going to the right, practically at a right angle to the line of play, caused by hitting the ball with the heel of the club.

SQUARE: a player who is square in relation to the target has his club face perpendicular to the line of play and his body aligned in parallel with that line of play.

STANCE: position of the feet on the ground. The stance can be: square (the line joining the ends of the feet is parallel with the line of play), closed (the tip of the left foot is slightly ahead of the line of play) or open (the tip of the right foot is a little ahead of the line of play).

SWAY: sideways movement of the player during the backswing with poor weight transfer.

SWING WEIGHT: balance point of a club. All the clubs in a set should have the same swing weight.

TAKEAWAY: the start of the backswing when the head of the club starts to move away from the ball.

TEE: small wooden or plastic peg pushed into the ground at the start of a hole, and on which the ball is placed; also the teeing off area of a hole. To tee: verb describing the action of inserting the tee.

TEMPO: rhythm of the swing.

TIMING: coordination of the different parts of the body while making the stroke.

TOP: a bad stroke, where the ball is struck on the top only. Its trajectory is along the ground.

TOPSPIN: forward spin on the ball – a lot of topspin makes the ball roll for a long time after it has landed on the ground.

WOOD: club with a solid wood or metal head. The most common type are woods numbered from 1 to 5. They are used to hit the ball long distances.

YIPS: trembling of the hands affecting the player and upsetting his putting.

ACKNOWLEDGMENTS
To French professionals and coaches,
in particular to Philippe Mendiburu,
one of the finest teachers.
To Dominic Nouilhac, a one-handicap golfer
at the Saint-Quentin-en-Yvelines golf course
who was good enough to pose
for all the technical tips photos

Translated by Liz Macdonald and edited by Nick Edmund
in association with First Edition Translations Ltd,
Cambridge, UK

Picture on p152-3 Joe Mann/Allsport

BIBLIOGRAPHY
Mon golf, Ken Bowden et Jack Nicklaus,
Office du livre, 1977.
The Fundamentals, Ben Hogan
Swing the handle, not the clubhead,
Eddie Merrins, GG.
Practical Golf, John Jacobs and Ken Bowden,
Stanley Paul, 1972.

MAGAZINES
Golf, Digest, USA
Golf-Magazine, USA
Golf Monthly, UK